Praise for *A God Who Hates*

"Wafa Sultan experienced firsthand the immense contempt of human dignity Islam harbors, and the unimaginable cruelty Muslim women have to endure on a daily basis resulting from it. Her compelling book is a touching life story filled with bone-chilling examples of what it is like to live in a society that is ruled by Islam and how valuable our Western freedom truly is. It is because brave women like Wafa Sultan have the courage to speak out against this doctrine of hate that we in the West have been forewarned. I hope that everyone reads this book and takes note of the important message it contains. We must defend our precious liberties, our Western freedom, and never give in to Islam."

—Geert Wilders, member of the
Dutch Parliament and leader of the Party for Freedom

"With rare courage and candor, Wafa Sultan throws open the shuttered windows on Islam, letting clean, bright sunshine pour into its darkest corners to illuminate Islam from the inside. This is where she lived it, confronted it, and ultimately rejected its sacralized teachings—on women, on marriage, on children, on Christians, on Jews, on freedom of conscience, on war, on world domination—as a humanity-warping pathology based on hate and fear. Such is the fascinating psychological analysis that is the underpinning achievement of *A God Who Hates*. With unique insight and unstinting compassion, Wafa Sultan, a trained psychiatrist, employs her expertise to put Islam on the couch. The results of her analysis will startle, engage, deepen, and transform every reader's understanding of Islam forever."

—Diana West, author of *The Death of the Grown-Up: How
America's Arrested Development
Is Bringing Down Western Civilization*

"Wafa Sultan paints a scorching, unforgettable portrait of Syrian Muslim society, especially the degradation of its women, and lyrically appreciates her adopted American homeland, which she calls 'the land of dreams.' But she also worries that Middle East customs are encroaching on the West and writes with passion to awaken Americans to a menace they barely recognize, much less fear." —Daniel Pipes, director of the Middle East Forum

"Like thousands of others, I first encountered Wafa Sultan on a stunning YouTube video. Here was a woman on Al Jazeera TV, eloquently and courageously defending Western civilization, individualism, and reason against the barbarity and mysticism of radical Islam. Her performance was mesmerizing. She was articulate, self-confident, and outspoken. She stunned the audience, the interviewer, and the pathetically outmatched Imam who opposed her. Now Wafa Sultan has written her life story in this powerful book. She exposes the ugliness that is Muslim society in the Middle East, while unapologetically defending the Western values she adopted when rejecting the religion of Islam. If you want to understand this courageous woman, who continues to fight for her beliefs in spite of death threats, and to understand her views on the conflict between Islam and the West, this is a must-read." —Yaron Brook, Ph.D., president and executive director of The Ayn Rand Institute

A God Who Hates

WAFA SULTAN

The Courageous Woman
Who Inflamed the Muslim World
Speaks Out Against the Evils of Islam

ST. MARTIN'S GRIFFIN

NEW YORK

AUTHOR'S NOTE

This is a true story, though some names have been changed.

A GOD WHO HATES. Copyright © 2009 by Wafa Sultan. All rights reserved.
Printed in the United States of America. For information, address St.
Martin's Press, 175 Fifth Avenue, New York, N.Y. 10010.

www.stmartins.com

Book design by Jonathan Bennett

The Library of Congress has cataloged the hardcover edition as follows:

Sultan, Wafa.
    A god who hates : the courageous woman who inflamed the Mus-
lim world speaks out against the evils of Islam / Wafa Sultan.—1st ed.
       p. cm.
    ISBN 978-0-312-53835-4
    1. Women in Islam. 2. Islam—Relations. 3. East and West.
I. Title.
    BP173.4.S848 2009
    297.082—dc22

                                      2009016930

ISBN 978-0-312-53836-1 (trade paperback)

D 10 9 8

To my dear husband and children
whose selfless love has sheltered me
when no other place seemed safe.

~

Lastly, to the memory of my beloved
niece Mayyada, who cut her life short
by committing suicide to escape the
hellish marriage imposed upon her
under Islamic Sharia Law: May her
tragic account be an eternal inspiration
to all who are privileged to live in free
societies. May her story encourage all
those who have been subjugated to
tyranny—especially women—to become
well informed and to persevere beyond
fear and intimidation. And a challenge:
To those whose spirits uphold the
principles of justice and freedom of
speech—May Mayyada's story, and that
of many more whose stories have never
been told, embolden you to speak up
against the unjust and immoral treatment of women in the Muslim world.

CONTENTS

ACKNOWLEDGMENTS

There is a saying in Arabic: "A single flower cannot create a blooming field." Likewise, without my many dedicated and supportive friends I would not have been able to bring this book to fruition. From the bottom of my heart, I would like to thank all and each one of them. I trust they know who they are; so, for me to mention their names is unnecessary. I do not wish to place their lives in danger in the same way my life is threatened.

Al Jazeera media network hosted me for three programs on their famous series, "*Al Itjah al Mouakes*" (The Opposite Direction). After the third interview, the station apologized to the Arab world for allowing me to "insult Islam" and as a consequence cancelled all rebroadcasts of the program. Nevertheless, my three interviews on Al Jazeera introduced me and my message to millions of people, and for that opportunity, I am wholeheartedly grateful to Al Jazeera.

Middle East Media Research Institute (MEMRI) played a major role in spreading my mission as well. For that I would like to extend my appreciation to them. MEMRI team labors diligently to break the language barriers in order to accurately

Acknowledgments

represent information emanating from the region and in doing so, offer an unbiased journalistic forum so the rest of the world may better appreciate the true nature of the perilous situation in the Middle East.

Finally, I would like to thank my dear readers in the Arab world whose responses, positive and negative, have encouraged me to persevere and overcome the grave challenges that must be faced in confronting hatred and religious intolerance.

A God Who Hates

WAFA SULTAN

*The Courageous Woman
Who Inflamed the Muslim World
Speaks Out Against the Evils of Islam*

ST. MARTIN'S PRESS 🐊 NEW YORK

I.

A God Who Hates

MOST MUSLIMS, IF not all of them, will condemn me to death
when they read this book. They may not even read it. The title
alone may push them to condemn me. That's how things are
with them. They don't read, or, if they do, they don't take in
what they read. They are much more interested in disagreement than in rapprochement and they are—first and foremost—
supremely interested in inducing fear in others with whom
they disagree. They may even threaten to condemn *you* just for
reading this book because, in their cruelty, they have learned
something about how to control others: Nothing tortures the
human spirit more effectively than making someone a prisoner
of her own fears. I am, though, no longer afraid. Why? Let me
tell you a fable that might explain how I confronted my fears of
speaking out against the radical mullahs of Islam.

There once was a strong and inquisitive young man who
loved to travel. In his thirst for knowledge, he moved from
place to place and traveled from town to town, drinking in wisdom and recording everything that happened to him.

Eventually, he came to a beautiful village slumbering at the
foot of a mountain surrounded on all sides by green hills where

gentle winds blew intermittently, delighting the mind and re-freshing the heart. In this beautiful place, he was shocked to see that the inhabitants of this village were sad. They moved slug-gishly, dragging their feet. To him they appeared no more than moving phantoms, without body or soul. The sight of these phantoms terrified him. He became determined to discover what made them so and set off to see a fabled wise man who lived alone, in a hut, cut off from the village and its inhabitants.

When he met the wise man, he asked what secret lay behind this great paradox. He asked why these people lived in a state of subjugation and dejection in a village where everything would seem to suggest that the people would be blessed with happi-ness and well-being. The sage came out of his hut and pointed toward the top of the mountain. "Look at that peak. An enor-mous ogre sits up there. From where he sits, he raves and shrieks, filling people's hearts with fear by threatening to gobble them up if they leave their homes or do any kind of work at all. The people, terrorized by his shrieks, can live only by stealth. Only their survival instinct keeps them going. They steal out like mice in secret to gather enough to keep body and soul to-gether. They live day by day, waiting impatiently for the mo-ment of their death. Their fear of this ogre has sapped their intellect and depleted their physical powers, reducing them to despair and hopelessness."

The young man thought for a while and said, "I'm going to the top of the mountain. I will talk to this ogre and ask what makes him threaten and frighten these people. I will ask him why he wants to prevent them from leading their lives in peace and safety."

"Go up to the top of the mountain? No sane person would

risk his life by daring to meet the ogre. I implore you not to do it for the sake of your life, young man!" But the young man would not be dissuaded. He was determined to do what he believed had to be done. And so, with slow but sure steps, he started on his way to the peak.

When the young man reached the peak, the ogre did, indeed, seem large at first; however, what he found as he walked on astonished him. The closer he got, the smaller the ogre became. By the time he arrived he found that this great ogre who terrorized many was smaller than his littlest finger. The young man flattened his hand, held out his palm, and the tiny ogre jumped onto it.

"Who are you?" the young man asked.

"I am Fear," the ogre replied.

"Fear of what?" the young man asked.

"That depends on who you are. How each person sees me depends on how he imagines me. Some people fear illness, and they see me as disease. Others fear poverty, so they see me as poverty. Others fear authority, so they see authority in me. Some fear injustice, others fear wild beasts or storms, so that's how I appear to them. He who fears water sees me as a torrent, he who fears war perceives in me an army, ammunition, and suchlike."

"But why do they see you as bigger than you really are?"

"To each person I appear as big as his fear. And as long as they refuse to approach and confront me they will never know my true size."

I sometimes feel like that young man, a person who rebels against the wisdom of her time. I once lived in a village much

like the one he discovered, for three decades. My love for it became an addiction from which I possessed neither the ability
nor the desire to escape. The ogre, for a time, held me in his
thrall, but no longer. Being enslaved to my own fears of the
demon was a terrible time in my life, but I don't regret the experience. For me, all things happen for a reason and that experience only made me stronger. I was not born in that village in
vain and I certainly did not leave it in vain. I left with a purpose
not unlike that of the young man. I feel, on most days, that I
must climb the mountain again and again with slow but sure
steps and confront that ogre who, for me, is the horror of radical Islam. I do it to show the people of that village how small
and cowardly he really is.

I have never in my life seen Muslims talk without disagreement. Perhaps I am alone in this, but I don't think so. If one
says "Good morning," the other will reply, "But it's nighttime
now." Their tendency to argumentativeness makes them defensive and their custom deems attack to be the best method of
defense since it gives them the chance to shout and shriek.
Shouting has become their hallmark and the main characteristic they use when they engage in conversation with someone
whom they don't agree with. Without it they have no sense of
their own worth or existence; without it they have no sense
even of being alive.

They concoct reasons for disagreement and welcome it much
more often than trying to bring different points of view closer
together. Why? Disagreement and confusion keeps the ogre big
and threatening, obscuring his true, puny nature. On top of
shouting their way through a conversation, they have acquired
the habit of shrieking, and they take pleasure in hearing their

own shrieks. They believe that the louder they shriek, the more they prove they are right. Their conversation consists of shouting, their talk is a screech, and he who shouts loudest and screeches longest is, they believe, the strongest. They fabricate disagreements so as to give themselves an opportunity to shout. They seek contradiction so that they can scream.

I have often wondered how this shrieking and shouting began and have had to think back to the roots of Islam to understand it. If you were lost in the desert, unable to distinguish between north or south, your life threatened by hunger, thirst, and heat, and surrounded by sand dunes on all sides with no sign in sight of a human being who could rescue you—at that moment, a scream is all you have to convince yourself that you are still alive. You scream in the hope that a passerby will hear.

Many Arab history books tell us stories of the terror and desolation people suffered in the desert. The one I think best depicts this situation is the story of the Bedouin whose only son fell ill and lay on his sickbed dying of fever. His father, overwhelmed with paternal pangs of helplessness, went out into the night in search of a doctor. He lost his way in the depths of the desert and wandered along not knowing where his feet were leading him until, after an immeasurable length of time, he saw from afar a faint light. He ran toward it, only to discover that it was the campsite he had left, and that his son had already departed this life.

This story and others like it, which abound in Arab literature, give us some idea of the harshness of the environment in which Islam was born and thrived. It was an arid environment in which death from hunger or thirst was a constant threat, and the struggle with it was savage. Confronted with it, men could acquire no skills to combat it, and the scream remained the only way to overcome this unyielding threat. The ability to scream settled deep into the unconscious mind of the Bedouin as their most important survival skill. Islam canonized the Muslims' desert nature, and from that moment on they were unable to acquire new ways of communicating with others. But, I wonder, why does this shrieking and shouting persist?

When a person adopts a particular style of behavior, he observes the degree to which other people accept it. If they encourage him, or at least make no objection, he will continue. The way the world has retreated, and continues to retreat, in the face of the Muslims' screams and shouts, has played a major role in encouraging them to continue to behave the way they do. When others remain silent or worse, retreat, Muslims get the impression that they are right. Their shrieks no longer affect me, and I no longer hear them. If one of them wants to talk to me—and I have no doubt that a small minority of them is made up of rational people—they will discover that I am genuinely open to dialogue; however, not a single one yet has stepped up to have a rational dialogue with me that doesn't include shouting and shrieking.

For me, someone who comes into this world without bequeathing a legacy leaves it without having fulfilled her purpose. Through looking at my childhood in that village and my departure for America I have tried to figure out why I was put on this earth. Every person can bring about change, and every change makes a difference. The world is a picture, and each person influences it, is influenced by it, and finally leaves a fresh mark upon it to give it new form. Those who do good works while they are on this earth beautify the picture. Those who do bad works disfigure it. I hope I was put here to do good works and beautify the picture.

The struggle between good and evil continues as long as the world goes on. I believe that good has prevailed, for the most part, and that it will continue to do so. The belief that evil will overrun the world is not the product of the twenty-first century. It has persisted everywhere at all times despite the fact that nothing could be further from the truth. Though the belief that evil has prevailed is groundless, I can understand why some people believe it. Evil shrieks loudly while goodness clothes the world in silence. It's easier to see the bad than the good. It is goodness, I believe, which has swept the world ever since the moment it came into being. Goodness, though, must be protected because if it is ever defeated by evil, our world will cease to exist. The wisdom of the age we live in cautioned me against writing this book and warned me that I might have to pay with my life for doing so, but I am undaunted. My belief that good will ultimately triumph over evil has encouraged me to speak out.

After the 9/11 terrorist attack Americans asked themselves: "Why do they hate us?"

My answer is: "Because Muslims hate their women, and any group who hates their women can't love anyone else."

People ask: "But why do Muslims hate their women?"

And I can only reply: "Because their God does."

Even men in my own family have caused sorrow in the lives of their women. How often have I dreamed of digging up my grandfather's bones so that I could bring him to trial for the misery he visited upon my grandmother? The times are too many to number. But I won't be able to exact vengeance for her, for Suha, for Samira, for Amal, for Fatima, or for the millions of other women living under the gaze of a hate-filled and vengeful god unless I expose what it is that really squats at the top of that mountain.

When a woman—oppressed to the very marrow of her bones, terrified by life in a village that confines her to a prison narrower than the eye of a needle—finally takes flight and escapes the clutches of its ogre, she finds herself and her three children alone and outcast in the streets of one of the largest cities in the world with only a hundred dollars in her pocket and a thousand years' worth of grief in her heart. This woman cannot speak the local language and she knows nothing of local customs and traditions. All she possesses is bitter experience whose depths cannot be plumbed without a great deal of courage. At one time, that woman was me.

When my feet touched the ground at the airport in Los Angeles, it was not just my family I was concerned for. I also worried about the people I left behind in my village. In Los Angeles, my first job was pumping gas at a gas station. On the very same day I started that job, I wrote my first article that dared to question and disagree with the shrieking mullahs and began to claw my way along two paths. The first was the path my family and I were traveling as we tried to earn enough to live and better ourselves. The other path I found myself on alone wound its way through the hills in my mind as I looked for a way to confront the ogre and free my family from his tyranny. What a difference there was between the two paths. The first was governed by law and morality and, however difficult, appeared possible. The other was ruled by the laws of the jungle, which can harm you, even in a civilized place like the United States.

Courage alone made me push forward along the mountain path with the same energy I devoted to making my way in a society that respected me, no matter what my weaknesses were. As a woman, the knowledge I now had access to because I was living in America satisfied my ravenous hunger to learn and released me from many of my fears and weaknesses. I was surrounded on all sides by books as I worked to better myself and my family. Books, so frequently denied to women in my culture, were the things that saved me. Once you arm yourself with books, you become ever more powerful—a bulldozer—and completing the journey, no matter how long and how difficult, never seems impossible.

After seventeen years in America, I've achieved the position I wanted in my new country. I've also become acquainted with a different God than the one I knew in my village. I can still see the woman who greeted me at the Los Angeles airport. So many years ago I set foot on American soil and this young woman, with a smile that still warms my heart, said, "Welcome to America!" No one had ever welcomed me anywhere before. The ogre, the old God I knew, had not only deprived me of my right to hear these words; he had also succeeded in convincing me that I was not worthy of possessing that right. America gave me back my right to live in a society that welcomed me, and showed me, for the first time, that I deserved that right.

I emerged from the Los Angeles airport that day with a new understanding that perhaps others have always known, but which I just understood because of the kindness of a woman

I'd never met before: People in every society worship their own image. Is the kind woman who welcomed me to Los Angeles not the God she worships? How much I wanted to exchange my ogre for her welcoming God at that very minute! I understood then that the God suits the person just as the lock suits the key. If a society has a defect, both lock and key have to be repaired. Fixing one or the other alone will not do. In my village, as in the America where I now live, the person is the God she worships. She regards that God as her ideal. She strives both consciously and unconsciously to draw closer to her ideal until she becomes one with it.

The woman at the Los Angeles airport gave me hope that people can change. Before a human being can change, however, the God he worships must be remolded. When I think of the waste of human life we see around us, I am disgusted. I am horrified by the waste of life that is the young Muslim who blows himself up in the midst of a crowd of schoolchildren. He kills twenty-eight people and himself because he is entirely deluded by the lie, forced on him by his God, that the deaths of these children will buy him entry to paradise and his houris. Isn't that young man striving to identify with that ogre, that God who hates, squatting on the hilltop in that melancholy village? Does he not hope to control and influence others through fear? If we want to transform others like the unfortunate young Muslim suicide bomber into reasonable human beings and preserve our world, we first have to help them see their ogre clearly and show them how to exchange their God who hates for one who loves.

2.

The Women of Islam

PEOPLE HAVE OFTEN asked me what turning point brought about the dramatic change which altered the course of my life. I believe my life really began in the third grade when I learned to read. From that point on, I developed an insatiable appetite for every book that came my way. By the time I got to the fourth grade, I was getting lost in *The Hunchback of Notre Dame, Gone with the Wind,* and the mysteries by Agatha Christie. My teachers, family, and family friends were generous in their attention and treated me as if I was a gifted child because of my precocious reading habits.

Even then, I loved to talk and talk and talk. I believe that the first thing that encouraged me to develop my talent for writing and public speaking was a comment made by my Arabic literature teacher. One day, in one of my exercise books he wrote, "I like your common sense and discernment. You have talent which you must nurture by reading until it matures. The road is a long one, but the fruit of the cactus emerges in all its sweetness from among the prickly spines." So, I was to be, with his encouragement, "the fruit of the cactus," the gift of a prickly plant, and his lines encouraged me to begin writing.

The way my family spoke about me provided the rest of the push I needed toward learning. When I heard my father talking about me, as he sat with his friends in the evenings, he sounded is if he were speaking of someone possessed of an unusually high degree of intelligence. I was embarrassed to hear him speak of me in that way. His lavish praise placed a great burden of responsibility on me and, from that moment on, I never wanted to disappoint him.

My maternal grandmother was my ideal and played a major role in my life. My most precious memory of her is the stories she would regale us with when we were little and gathered around her every evening. She showed me the worth of a woman, as well as how one could be trod under the heels of one's husband in the Muslim world. She was a strong woman, and, had she been allowed the opportunities I enjoyed, she would have been the Arabic Margaret Thatcher. She was also a sad woman who could be harsh, but for a long time, I never knew the secret that lay behind the profound sadness in her eyes. By the time she was in her early twenties she already had three sons and two daughters. A smallpox epidemic swept through her village and carried off a large number of its inhabitants. It stopped at her door and took away her three sons, leaving only her daughters. My grandfather awoke in the night to find himself enveloped not in sadness, but in shame. He had become a "father of daughters," and, of course, my grandmother was held responsible for his disgrace, as she had borne him those daughters.

My grandfather was the local *mukhtar*—the head of the village—and his position did not permit him to remain without sons. Since he held my grandmother responsible for his disgrace, within a week of the death of her sons, my grandfather forced my grandmother to approach one of the village's best-known families and ask for their beautiful daughter's hand in marriage . . . for him. By her own accounts, my grandmother made a very good job of describing to the new bride my grandfather's virtues as a man of distinction and she returned home with the family's consent.

It was the custom for the bride to ride to the bridegroom's home on a horse led by a member of her family. She would be met by a woman from the bridegroom's family who would welcome the bridal procession by dancing before it with a bowl of incense on her head. The bride would reward the woman by throwing a few coins into the bowl. My grandfather, without a thought for my grandmother's feelings, insisted that she carry the bowl and perform the dance before the bridal procession. He forced the woman who bore five of his children to denigrate herself before others in the village for the simple and selfish reason than that he didn't want the few coins his new bride would toss into the bowl to go to anyone outside the family.

My grandmother swallowed her pride and hid her sadness away to perform the dance. At the end of the wedding ceremony she felt that, although she might have lost her husband, she had at least gained a golden Ottoman pound. Her happiness about even that small triumph was short-lived. At dawn that first day, she awoke to the sound of a gentle knocking at the door of her room. When she spied my grandfather through a crack in the door she was thunderstruck. In a low voice he whispered in her ear, "My bride is still asleep, and I'm here to borrow the golden pound. I promise I'll give it back to you when we bring in the harvest at the end of the season."

My grandmother gave him the coin and went back to bed

empty-handed, deprived of everything except her sadness. After the wedding, my grandmother was reduced to the status of a servant in her own home. She served my grandfather, his wife, and the ten boys that wife would bear for him. My grandmother accepted this humiliation, swallowed the insult, and worked from dawn till dusk in the house and the fields, all for the sake of her daughters. Some fifty years later my grandfather died without having given my grandmother back her pound. My grandmother died about fifteen years after that, still insisting— as a loyal Muslim wife must—that her husband had been a man of distinction, just as she had when he forced her to solicit a young woman to become his new bride.

A Muslim woman does not usually have the right to choose anything about her life; but in the rare circumstance that she does, that woman does not hesitate for a moment in choosing what suits her, even if she has to pay a price for that choice. When my mother married, my grandmother decided to escape the hell of life with my grandfather and moved in with her brother and his family. Although her life with her brother was little better, she felt that by leaving home she had taken a stand against her husband. After my mother's marriage, she began to fuss over the children like a broody hen. My father's five children from his first wife lived with us. I was the fourth of my mother's eight offspring. When I came into the world I had to compete for a foothold in a house that swarmed with children. Several years after my mother's marriage, my father asked my grandmother to come and live with us so that she could help my mother with the housework and the children. In the Arab world it is not usual for a woman to live in her son-in-law's home and my grandmother agreed to my father's request so as to make a point with her brother just as she had with my grandfather: She could make a choice. Life in our house was different for my grandmother. My father treated my grandmother with respect and seized every opportunity to praise her hard work and her role in raising the children. In his house, my grandmother breathed the fresh air of freedom and showered us with love and tenderness.

My mother was different. She did not share my grandmother's ability to cast off the effects of her past, and was always a sad, angry, and stubborn woman. My father was dazzled by her youthful beauty as a child is dazzled by a toy. He was about twenty-five years older than she was. She was younger than his eldest daughter. He treated her well, but even this could not bring a smile to my mother's face. The age difference between them was too great and their betrothal had not been her choice.

My father was a businessman who was respected and well known in the town where we lived. He was a grain merchant who sold the product of crops grown in eastern Syria to buyers in the coastal area. He provided us with a standard of living that many families in our region could not even dream of at the time. His day began at four o'clock in the morning when he would get up and make the morning coffee. Within a few moments the scent of Turkish coffee would pervade every corner of the house. Still half asleep, I would see him approach my mother's bed and whisper quietly in her ear, "Coffee's ready, dearest." But she would thrust him away with a shove and he would go back to his chair on the veranda overlooking the sea, and, on most occasions, drink his coffee alone.

One of my happiest memories of him is of his return from a

long journey at his usual dawn hour, when he would run to his family and wake us all up shouting, "Come on out, and bring bags with you!" We would run outside, pushing and shoving, and then race to the grain truck that stood blocking the street in front of our house. The driver would help us carry in the bags full of sweets, fruit, and vegetables. In the melon and watermelon season, we would compete to see who could carry the most.

My father spent very little time at home. He would leave in the morning before sunrise and come home after dark. In his absence my grandmother reigned supreme. Our town suffered from a shortage of schools. To solve this problem, each school had two shifts of pupils. On Saturdays, Sundays, and Mondays, the girls went to school from seven in the morning until noon, while the boys started their school day at half past twelve and studied until five o'clock in the evening. This arrangement was reversed on the remaining three school days, Tuesday, Wednesday, and Thursday, when the boys started school in the mornings, while the girls studied in the afternoons. On the days I went to school in the afternoon I would accompany my grandmother to the local market in the early morning to buy the day's necessities.

My grandmother's village, where she lived until the day she left her brother's house for my father's, is about seven miles away from the town where we lived. For twenty years after the day she left it, she never set foot there again. I remember the first time she went back after those twenty years, to attend the funeral of one of her sisters. My grandmother clearly loved the village she grew up in, but she had an astonishing capacity for concealing her feelings. Occasionally, I would get a glimpse of these emotions when I accompanied her on her morning excursions to the market in our own town.

Near the market there was a bus station and taxi rank where people gathered to wait for transport to the surrounding villages. In one of the corners stood a kiosk that sold falafel sandwiches, plates of hummus, and fava beans. It was owned by a relative of my grandmother's who came from the same village as she did. My grandmother loved falafel and she would make straight for the kiosk every morning. Then she would begin to chat with her relative Muhammad the falafel seller and embark upon a long conversation with him, in the course of which he would inform her of every incident, large and small, which had occurred in her village. The time my grandmother spent in these conversations with Muhammad gave me some of my most precious moments.

That rubbish bin behind Muhammad's kiosk was the first school I graduated from. Muhammad would wrap the falafel sandwiches in pages torn from magazines, books, and newspapers that he bought for a trifling sum from people who had finished reading them. Behind the kiosk was the bottom half of a large barrel that was used for rubbish, and Muhammad's customers would throw their sandwich wrappings into it when they had finished eating.

While my grandmother was busy talking, I would sneak up to the barrel and climb onto the stone wall that ran alongside it. Then I would bend over, inclining my skinny body until I could reach inside and pick out the pages. I would scrape the remains of the sesame paste and falafel off them, smooth them flat, then fold them carefully and hide them in my pockets and underneath my jacket to read later. I would continue retrieving those pages that were precious to me until I heard my grandmother's voice shouting, "Where have you got to, you little monkey? Playing in the rubbish? What a dirty little girl!" Then she would give me the rest of her sandwich and I would devour it inspired by the thought of the damp papers filling my pockets. Those visits to Muhammad's falafel stand gave me my first access to the contents of the free Lebanese press and, consequently, the European and French newspapers it replicated. At the end of the 1960s when I was growing up, the Arabic newspaper market was dominated by the free Lebanese press. This was especially true of Syria. The freedom I saw being exercised in that press system inspired me. The newspaper pages I retrieved from Muhammad's rubbish bin represented a freedom of thought and expression largely unknown in the Arabic world and they made me bold, made me look for the truth in all things.

On Fridays, our day off, I would spend most of the day copying the pages I had found into a special exercise book that I kept after I had thrown the dirty bits of paper into the wastebasket. Not a week passed without my discovering pages from one newspaper or another. The *Reader's Digest,* in its Arabic-language version *Al-Mukhtar,* was the only object of my search that did not find its way into Muhammad's barrel. Unfortunately, its small pages could not be wrapped around the sandwiches. As a result, buying *Reader's Digest* mercilessly devoured two weeks' pocket money every month, but I didn't mind. What I found there was more than worth the drain on my allowance.

Through the *Reader's Digest* I learned about the United States, the country of Uncle Sam. Up to that point, I imagined the United States as existing on a planet quite different from the one I inhabited. In its pages I first encountered the Statue of Liberty and, in the early years of my life, tried to assume her personality. I imagined that if I were that woman, the very first thing I would do would be to put a smile on my mother's face and write a ferocious letter to my grandfather, finally telling him off for the despicable way in which he treated my grandmother. I won't deny, though, that my initial reaction toward this statue was a feeling of envy. Why could she carry a torch in one hand and a book in the other and stand haughtily in public view without fear or embarrassment, and I couldn't? My whole life, both then and now, has been an attempt to answer that question.

I saw this statue of a woman who was my rival and whose enthusiasm for books I imagined matched my own for the first time from the window of a Pan American plane which bore me through the skies over New York as I arrived from Frankfurt on December 25, 1988. My heart leapt for joy at the sight of her and my envy evaporated at once, to be replaced, I don't know from where, by a sense of security and triumph. I had a six-hour wait at New York airport before I could board the plane to Los Angeles where my husband would be waiting for me. On the flight from New York to Los Angeles I wrote a letter to my grandfather, by then already in his grave, in which I vented my anger toward him; by the time my feet touched the ground of Los Angeles I felt that my load had been lightened, even though I was unable to put a smile on my grandmother's face.

In a country like mine, oppressed people feel as if fate is against them. It wasn't just men who were the enemy of my mother, my grandmother, and every other woman in the country. Women usually also blamed fate for their ill luck and on June

14, 1967—the tenth day of the cease-fire on the Syrian-Israeli front in the Six-Day War—fate came knocking at our door. My father went to eastern Syria to bring back a load of grain and never came home. It was nighttime and there was no traffic on the road. On the six-hundred-mile journey, for some reason I have never been able to discover, his truck overturned in a deep ravine in the mountain range between coastal and central Syria. My father bled for hours. A military truck came down that road bringing the body of a Syrian soldier home to his village in the mountains. The driver saw my father's truck lying overturned in the gully and stopped at once. He took my father and his driver to the hospital in the town nearby. The driver survived, but my father died from an internal hemorrhage.

My father's death turned our lives upside down. My mother was in her early thirties and had lost the little sense she had left to her. My half-brother, my father's only son from his first wife, intervened and took the place of my father in our lives. He was, like my father, affectionate and warmhearted, and he showered us with kindness. He took over the running of my father's business and struggled to maintain a good standard of living for both our family and his own—for he was already the father of six children.

My experience of life in his house was the thing that began to form my political beliefs. My brother was a member of the Syrian National Party, and this fact was largely responsible for his indifference toward Islam. He wasn't against it, but he wasn't for it, either! One of the items on the party agenda was the struggle for Arab unity and the creation of a single Arab nation irrespective of religious allegiance. The Islamists regarded this as a threat to Islam, which strives to create a single nation founded on religious adherence to comprise all Muslims, Arab and non-Arab. The unseen struggle between these two opposing camps caused supporters of the National Party to adopt a covertly hostile attitude toward religion in general and Islam in particular, freeing them from the constraints of Muslim teaching.

My brother never openly showed his dislike of the Islamists, but, as I said, he did not care for them. He was well aware that Islam was the burial ground of any attempt to move the Arab-speaking countries forward toward progress. His political position helped broaden the way he thought about things and it subsequently affected the way he treated me as his sister and as a woman. He respected my opinions from the start, and allowed me a greater degree of freedom than most Muslim women in the region could ever dream of knowing.

Oddly, it was my grandmother—the woman whom I idolized—who tried hardest to persuade me of the truth of the traditional image of women as creatures unfit to look after themselves. Encouraged by her, each of my young brothers attempted to take control of my life and assume the role of protective male toward me. But their wishes frequently conflicted with those of my half-brother, who wanted me to enjoy a relatively large degree of freedom. As he was the eldest, their desires took second place to his. He often intervened on my behalf to protect me from their aggressive behavior and their attempts to exert authority over me.

During the period between my father's death and the day I graduated from high school, I was comparatively free. I was allowed to go to the cinema and see most of the Egyptian movies that then dominated the Arabic film industry, and permitted to read most books, magazines, and newspapers. I can remember numerous occasions, when, for one reason or another, I had a run-in with one of my brothers, who would then rain down blows upon me. My shrieks—like those of the Bedouin—were usually my only means of defense, as my high-pitched voice was much more powerful than my small body.

My grandmother would quickly stick her fingers in her ears to shut out the noise, saying, "May God quiet her voice! It goes right through you. You shameless girl! So your brother gave you a slap in the face—what's the problem? He's just disciplining you. Has the Kaaba* collapsed?"

"Has the Kaaba collapsed?" That question still echoes in my head. Time after time, though I worshipped her, I wanted to shout in my grandmother's face: "Shut up, you stupid woman! You may have let my grandfather beat you, but I am not going to let anyone hit me. A man hitting me is a much more serious matter than the collapse of the Kaaba!" My deep love and respect for her, along with our traditions which forbid us to defy those older than ourselves, held me back.

Because I passed my school graduation exams with distinction, I was eligible for medical school. I had no ambitions of becoming a doctor and never dreamed of practicing medicine. I dreamed of studying Arabic literature so as to one day be able to write flawless Arabic, but I excelled at mathematics, biology, physics, and other scientific subjects. Giving up on medicine, then, would have disappointed my family. Out of respect

---

Kaaba: a Muslim shrine in Mecca toward which Muslims turn to pray.

for my brother's pride in my achievements, I gave in and agreed without protest to go to medical school as he wanted me to.

I moved from Baniyas to Aleppo, so that I could attend Aleppo University. Life in Aleppo, the second largest city in Syria after its capital Damascus, was noisy and very different from life in Baniyas, which was a small quiet town slumbering on the shores of the Mediterranean. In Aleppo I found myself all alone in a society quite unlike the one in which I had been born and raised. Baniyas's proximity to the sea had made it accessible to European tourism and kept it comparatively free of the constraints of Islamic law, which shackled the lives of the inhabitants of Aleppo.

In Aleppo I was the guest of a local Muslim family. My brother had met Ahmad, the husband, through his work, and they had become friends. Ahmad insisted that I live with them during the term as I was considered too young to live on my own and my brother agreed. Ahmad's wife, a young woman in her mid-twenties, welcomed me as a heaven-sent distraction from her cares, as she had never before met a fellow Muslim woman who did not cover her head and whose family allowed her to live on her own in a strange town far from home. The couple had two small children, but I got as much attention from the friend and his wife as they did.

Staying with them showed me a way of life I had never known before. Islamic teachings reigned supreme over everything that went on in the house. I quickly realized how lucky my grandmother had been, even in her terrible marriage to my grandfather, when I compared it with the life this young woman led and the relationship she had with her husband, a short, bald, coarse-featured man with skinny limbs and a pendulous belly.

She was a very beautiful woman, with green eyes, fair pinkish skin, and long blond hair.

I once asked her, "Why did you choose him?"

She laughed and said, "Choose him? Me? Where are you from—Switzerland?"

And, indeed, she did regard me as a woman from another planet. Her name was Huda, and when she was sixteen years old a woman came knocking on her family's door looking for a girl of marriageable age. As soon as the woman laid eyes on Huda she was struck by her beauty and immediately asked her mother for her hand in marriage as a bride for her son. After meeting the man's family, Huda's father seized this opportunity to marry his daughter off to this wealthy man, even though the prospective groom was fourteen years older than she was.

It was not until her wedding night that she saw the bridegroom for the first time. When he came into her room she began to shudder. The wedding guests were all waiting outside the door for proof of her virginity. The bridegroom fell upon her like an animal and emerged from the room a few minutes later bearing a piece of cloth stained with her blood. The female members of the family shouted for joy and danced.

She confessed to me more than once that she did not love her husband, and that she was, in fact, very much afraid of him— but she had no other options. She never left the house unless he escorted her. They lived in a traditional quarter where everyone remained behind closed doors. I never saw a single open window in the entire neighborhood the whole time I stayed with them.

He would pick a quarrel with her on the slightest pretext, or for no reason at all. She would take very good care not to utter a single word when he was angry. Anything she said would be used against her. Often I would come out of my room and find myself confronting him as I defended her. When we argued he would quote from the Koran and the sayings of the Prophet in order to justify his behavior and assert his right to mistreat his wife. But I forced him to respect me, and he was afraid of my sharp tongue. He was also terrible at holding his own in an argument and, when confronted with me and the way I steam-roll others (yes, I know I do . . .), he would smooth things over by saying, half jokingly, half seriously, "You'll end up in hell, because you don't follow the teachings of Islam."

The oldest of their two children was five years old and his brother was a year younger, yet the husband used both boys to spy on his wife. The older boy clearly understood the type of relationship his parents had and manipulated them both. From my room I would often hear his mother shouting, "Wafa, I need your help—come here and be my witness," and I would find the elder boy threatening his mother and telling her that, if she didn't do what he wanted, he would tell his father that she had spoken to a man on the phone, opened the door to someone, or left the house.

I lived with them for one whole school year. In my second year, unable to stand being a witness to the household sadness any longer, I moved into university accommodation and stayed there until I graduated from medical school. I stayed in touch with Huda and her family, however, because I felt sorry for her, and visited her at least twice a week. During those years I was able to observe firsthand the crime against humanity—against both men and women—that was being perpetrated in Ahmad and Huda's home, which to a great extent was representative of how people in Aleppo lived. The teachings of Islam have destroyed the men and women there, and rendered them incapable of the smallest measure of humane behavior.

Ahmad, with his violent and cruel behavior toward his wife, fell into the same category as my grandfather. I hated him. I began to question things I had always seen as certainties. The worldview I had developed growing up in Baniyas began to be eroded as doubts about Islam and its teachings grew stronger. The time I spent in Aleppo, and my experiences with Ahmad's family in particular, heralded a new stage in my life that formed most of my subsequent convictions and attitudes regarding Islam.

3·

Finding Hope for the Men of Islam

IN THE SUMMER of 1977 I met a gynecologist through Ahmad. When this doctor learned that I was a fourth-year medical student he asked if I would like to work with him for a few hours a day in his clinic in a crowded, traditional suburb. I welcomed the suggestion and started work at once. In his clinic I came face to face with all those things that had been hidden behind the closed doors and windows of Ahmad's home and neighborhood. My work at this clinic was confined, in most cases, to diagnosing pregnancies and confirming the virgin status of young girls. Most of the girls were unmarried and came with their mothers or grandmothers who wanted to reassure them-selves that their daughter or granddaughter was a virgin, and some also came to find out if they were pregnant. It was the doctor's task to abort the children of the girls who were preg-nant and patch up those who had lost their virginity.

The patients and their escorts entered the office concealed under their cloaks so that only their hands showed. None wished to risk being recognized. In the examination room, where the woman and her daughter or granddaughter talked to the doc-tor, the story was always the same: "Doctor, my daughter had a serious fall and bled when she was a child, and we're here now to make sure she's still a virgin, because she's about to get married."

When the doctor explained, after examining the young girl, that she hadn't just lost her virginity but was also pregnant, the two women would weep and beg the doctor to help solve their problem.

In most cases, after a number of questions, the young woman would confess that for many years, since childhood, she had been sexually abused by her father, her brother, an uncle, or another male relative. Frequently, the girl had only just begun to menstruate and had become pregnant not long after her first period. One would think that a doctor's attitude to young women in distress such as this would have been one of care and sympathy. No relationship between a man and a woman in that sick society could be anything but oppressive and exploitative, not even the relationship between a male doctor and his female patients. The doctor frequently took advantage of the sensitivity of the situation and demanded fantastic sums as payment. The two women would come back the next day with the money, which they might have obtained by selling some of their jewelry. Watching this whole seedy drama play out, I was just as sickened by the doctor's attitude as I was by the abuse—sexual and otherwise—these women were suffering at the hands of their male relatives.

Outside the gynecologist's office, things were no better for women and I found myself experiencing some of this abuse firsthand. The university was situated outside the town, and the journey from the campus to the town center was one of the most difficult treks a female student had to make, at least twice a week, in order to buy our weekly supplies.

This journey, which took about an hour by bus, was a cruel one. The bus route passed through many neighborhoods and only ten minutes after leaving the campus the vehicle would already be packed with passengers crammed in like sardines. Most of the women on the bus, who never made up more than a quarter of the total number of passengers, were students, and their movements resembled those of mice attempting to flee from a malicious cat. No sooner did a man get the opportunity to press up against a woman than his penis would poke into her back like an iron bar. Shrieked complaints could be heard, but the sad fact of the matter was that the residents of the town regarded the female students as prostitutes, plain and simple.

Once out of the bus and on to the street, it was not much better. The contempt displayed toward us was nonstop. It was nerve-racking and exhausting to be in any public place any day of the week, if you were a woman. Friday, though, was the most difficult day and we avoided going out in public at all. The buses and streets were full of men on their way to the mosques. Any one of them who had the good fortune to be able to press up against a young woman, even if only for a few moments, had enough time to ejaculate in his pants so that he could arrive at the mosque to stand before his god in a more gratified frame of mind.

On Fridays I would usually have lunch with Ahmad and Huda and their family and spend the rest of the day with them indoors. Often I would get into vehement arguments with them over the backwardness of the local population.

Huda would usually remain quiet while Ahmad made his way from one Koranic verse to the next and quoted one saying of the Prophet after another in order to demonstrate the truth of his beliefs, while impugning the morals of every woman who lived, like me, far from her family. I refused to back down, however, and from that time on I learned to defend myself stubbornly and determinedly. It was also the time that I discovered how impudent and easily defeated the men of my society were.

Together with Ahmad and his family I attended a number of weddings in the town. Rather than being happy affairs, they provided me with another opportunity to explore more deeply this society, which appeared to be sick to the very marrow of its bones. At weddings people would split up into two groups, with the women in one room and the men in another. Each group celebrated in its own way. Women wore the most striking clothes and remarkable finery to these weddings. Their clothing, however, was not the only thing that was shocking. Normally staid, the women became voracious. I had never seen anything like it in my life. Women would go up to one another and touch each other in an unnatural manner, such as pinching a bottom or a breast, or putting a hand between thighs. None of them appeared surprised by this behavior, nor did anyone protest against it. Toward the end of the wedding celebration an announcement would be made that the bridegroom was on his way to the women's hall to collect his bride. As soon as they heard this, the women would quickly pick up their wraps and would transform themselves within minutes into objects resembling rubbish bins arrayed along a highway, each indistinguishable from the next. They went from being as beautiful as

Scheherazade to as ugly as what can only be called a human garbage can in a matter of minutes, trained by a sick society to cover a body they were told would lead men astray.

Only a trip to Damascus gave me hope for the men of Islam. In my second year, on Good Friday, my roommate Siham invited me to go on a trip to Damascus with her and a group of students from the agricultural union. I insisted on staying with my youngest half-sister, who lived in the capital and was married to a high-ranking officer in the Syrian army. We arrived at night, and the trip's organizer suggested sending one of the young men to escort us and ensure that we arrived safely at my sister's home. My sister, her husband, and their children were waiting for my roommate and me at the supper table. When my brother-in-law opened the door he welcomed us and insisted that our escort come in and share our evening meal.

The young man got into a political conversation with my brother-in-law and, after he had left, my brother-in-law turned to us and said, "He seems a well-educated young man and knows more about politics than one would expect of someone of his age and experience." I didn't give it or the young man another thought.

Damascus is a beautiful and ancient city whose sights have always enchanted me and I spent my time looking out of the windows on both sides of the bus, ignoring the chatter of my fellow students. The young stranger, who had dined with us at my sister's house, kept following me around. Given what I knew of Muslim men, I couldn't put enough distance between the two of us.

Once the weekend was over and we were back in Aleppo,

Siham went to visit her family in her home town. I was sitting alone in my room when the bell rang. I went down to the ground floor only to find the young man who had followed me around throughout our visit to Damascus. I wondered, "Is he stalking me?," as I greeted him, and he proceeded to show me photographs he had taken on the trip. Getting more and more nervous, not being able to figure out what he wanted, I stammered, "Siham's not here, but I'll give her the pictures as soon as she gets back." He answered, "I haven't come to see Siham. I came to see you, and I brought copies of the pictures as a present for you because you're in some of them."

All of a sudden, I didn't know what was happening to me. Before he had finished speaking, I felt a shock, an electric current flowing through my body. This was the first time in my life as a Muslim woman that I had talked alone with a young man. I was embarrassed and flustered and I asked him to follow me to the students' cafeteria where we could have tea.

I shall never forget that meeting as long as I live. His name was Morad and he was to become my husband and the father of my children. We met in defiance of the custom that does not permit a young girl to sit in a public place with a young man she does not know. For those few minutes I felt that I was the one breaking with tradition, the one who was more responsible for breaking the rule than he was and it brought with it a sense of sin. But, it was wonderful talking with him over tea, looking at the pictures and, after that, we began to spend more time together. We always met in public places, such as the university cafeteria or the bus, which took us from the campus to the center of town and back again. My relationship with Morad changed my life in Aleppo. It grew to be such a big part of my life that it became difficult to conceal it from Ahmad, Huda, and their family and therein lay the greatest obstacle we faced, for they tried to interfere in every detail of my life as soon as they learned of my relationship with Morad. They threatened to tell my brother and my family, and I—in my usual defiant way—dared them to carry out their threat.

Although Morad was a native of Aleppo and had lived there all his life, he remained an individual who existed apart from the town. His father had been a soldier in the French army during the French occupation of Syria. When the French forces left Syria in 1947, the newly established Syrian national army retained many of the French-trained soldiers but demobilized the older men, including his father. Morad was born in 1953. His father, over forty years old at the time, was delighted at the birth of this first son after two daughters. His father had a friend named George who lived in a neighborhood distant from their own, and this friend happened to be a Christian. George started a business and gave my husband's father a job as a salesman. The friendship grew as a foundation of mutual trust and respect developed between the two men. For reasons of which my husband is still unaware, his father sensed that his end was near and asked his friend George to take care of his only son should anything happen to him.

His father's intuitions turned out to be well founded: He died from a heart attack in 1956 when my husband was three years old. His eldest sister married at the age of thirteen, a few months before their father's death, while the younger sister married a year after his death, when she was eleven. And so, at the age of three, my husband was left to live alone with his mother.

My husband's mother, from his description of her, was an

eccentric woman with a vicious tongue and an unbalanced personality. She fought with George, whom she accused alternately of fraud and greed. Nonetheless, George stuck to the instructions that my husband's father had given him and insisted on assuming a paternal role, despite the difficulties involved in dealing with Morad's mother. He used to visit them at least twice a week, bringing presents. George, in his suit, tie, and small felt cap stood out as an obvious Christian among the men of my husband's childhood quarter, all of whom were Muslim. As a young boy my husband welcomed and enjoyed George's visits, but at the same time, they were always a source of shame and embarrassment to him. All the local children were Muslim, and they showed him no pity, repeating in his hearing what they heard at home. My husband, as a child, could not bear their constant questioning: "Who's that Christian?," "Why do you let him and his family visit you?," "Aren't you afraid that he'll convert you to Christianity?"

The hatred of Christians by the Muslim community and his fondness for George played on my husband's young mind and his mother used that growing conflict to damage him in a way that only a cruel mother can. As a young widow with limited capabilities living in a society which preys upon its women, she aggravated his sense of shame. When his father died, the family was living in a small wood-and-metal house of the kind left behind by the French army, in an area far from the center of town. After the French left and the Syrian national army had taken control of the barracks, people moved out of these houses, which with time fell into ruin, while their own small homes remained standing among the rubble in an uninhabited military zone about two miles from the nearest residential area. After she was widowed, my husband's mother had to go out to work in a tobacco factory, leaving home early in the morning and returning only after dark. But when she did come home, her hurtful tongue worked to destroy him, showering him with curses and hitting him as punishment for some task undone. Blind to her son's already fragile state of mind, she used him as her whipping boy.

As in most cities, what we now call "gentrification" took over and Aleppo's wealthy residents, on the lookout for less-crowded localities, were quick to move into the area around my husband's home. The school nearest their house filled up with the children of very wealthy families, and he stuck out among them like a sore thumb. The class differences crushed him. He remembers his mother saying to him: "The houses will creep toward us until the time comes when we are pushed out with nowhere to go but the street." To this day, whenever he sees a homeless person he hides his face in his hands so as not to imagine himself in his place.

On his mother's days off, when he would accompany her on shopping expeditions to the local market, he was hurt by the way the stallholders treated her, no matter how cruel she was to him. They took advantage of her foolishness and the fact that she was a woman in a male environment. They overcharged her, and when she tried to bargain with them and accused them of swindling her, they would abuse her, using language which my husband's young ears could not bear. It was as if they were shouting at her: "Go home and hide yourself away, you shameless creature! Where's your husband, and how can he allow you to wander around among men like this?" Morad discovered at a very early age the true nature of the world in which he lived and was never able to truly become part of it. His sympathies lay with his mother, the cruel woman who corrupted his own mind, who he saw clearly as a victim of Muslim society.

In high school, he joined the Baath Party, which was trying to recruit the largest possible number of high-school students, and those who came from poor families were the most eager to join. He was attracted to the party because it was a secular organization that—at least on the face of it—attached no importance to religion. The party's slogans gave them the illusion of hope for a better life and equal opportunities. While still an adolescent he plunged headlong into the political activism of the group and, working with other party members, slowly began to find himself. After school he would go straight to meetings with fellow party members. He had now found what life with his mother had so long denied him. He now had something to live for. The party's slogans and agenda imbued him with anti-Semitism and incited him against Israel. Brainwashed by the sick culture he had been taken into, he began to believe that killing Jews and throwing them into the sea was his sole reason for living.

He continued to live with his mother but dwelt in his own private world, a world in which he dreamed of a job that would allow him to support himself rather than having to wait for his mother to come home with eggs and bread. He graduated from high school and went to university to study agricultural engineering. He found work as a teacher's aide in a primary school, though one thing clouded his happiness as a teacher: the fact that at least an hour a day had to be devoted to teaching the Muslim religion.

When he asked Christian pupils to leave the classroom while

this class was in progress, he felt that he was forfeiting his humanity. Many parents complained to the school administration of his shortcomings as a teacher of religious education, but he turned a deaf ear to them as he knew that his membership in the Baath Party put him in a strong position, and these complaints did not cause him to lose a single day's work. In those days Islam took second place to the Baath Party. From the late 1960s until the mid-1970s Syria went through a phase in which Islam almost entirely lost its influence, at least over schoolchildren and university students. In the mid-1970s the tentacles of the Saudi octopus began to extend gradually into Syrian public life, where they still wreak havoc today.

Morad had a difficult life and I knew that the best thing I could do for him was just to listen carefully anytime he was able to share a painful memory. Once, he said to me, "Listen, Wafa! A woman—my mother—destroyed me, and now I'm looking for another woman—a wife—who can put the pieces back together again! My mother was very well able to demolish me, and I believe that you are just as able to put me back together." I'm still in the process of trying to put him back together again. I know that many sardonic women joke about this, but I really did marry a wreck of a man who was destroyed by his mother. I'm still trying to repair him. I don't bear Morad's mother the slightest grudge, as I don't consider her responsible for the way she made him suffer. She was merely a victim of her society and its belief system, and my husband was this victim's own victim.

4.

A Quest for Another God

IN MY FIFTH year at university, in 1979, something happened that changed my life. That year a violent and bloody struggle broke out between the Syrian authorities, as embodied in the ruling family and its dependents, and the terrorists of the Syrian Muslim Brotherhood. The Syrian president belongs to the Alawite Muslim community, a minority that derives its name from that of Ali, the Prophet Muhammad's cousin and the fourth caliph to rule after his death. The Alawites constitute between 15 percent and 20 percent of the Syrian population and are the largest Muslim group in the country after the Sunni majority. The Alawite Hafez al-Assad came to power in the wake of a military coup. He was minister of defense at the time.

Throughout Muslim history the Alawites were the poorest members of Syrian society. Before the Ottoman occupation of Syria, the overwhelming majority of Alawites lived in Aleppo, the town I lived in as a medical student in the north of the country, near the Turkish border. When the Ottoman forces swept through northern Syria they butchered the Alawites, killing most of them. Those who survived fled toward the coast, and eventually settled in the mountains between central Syria and the sea. The deep gullies and tortuous winding terrain of that arid mountain region provided a refuge for the scattered remnant of the fleeing Alawites, who hid in its caves.

In their new habitat the Alawites suffered appalling poverty, neglect, and oppression at the hands of both the Ottoman occupiers and the Sunni majority. Under the French Mandate of Syria they breathed more easily, as it granted them a measure of autonomy.

When the last French forces pulled out of Syria in 1946 the Alawites found themselves worse off than they had been under Ottoman rule. Between 1946, when Syria became independent, and 1963, when the Baath Party came to power, the Alawites suffered cruel hardships and ill-treatment. Besieged in their mountain caves they led primitive lives little different from those of people in the Stone Age. No roads linked them to the Syrian coastal towns. Fear that they would be killed, their women raped, and their livestock and crops pillaged kept them confined within their mountain fortress.

The Baath Party was founded by a group of Syrians— mainly Christians and Alawites—who belonged to the country's educated elite. The party came into being, in fact, as a reaction against the religious and social persecution that Syrian minorities suffered at the hands of the Sunni majority, and these Muslim and non-Muslim minorities were the main beneficiaries of its founding. For a considerable time after they came to power in 1963, the Baathists made a genuine attempt to rid Syria of its social distinctions and class differences, providing new work opportunities for many, without discrimination. Its original aim was the establishment of a secular Syrian state whose slogan was "religion for God and the homeland for everyone." Young Alawites soon discovered the Baath Party as a new way of escaping their hardship and poverty and they joined in huge numbers. Some were lucky enough to attain high positions, and Hafez al-Assad, a prominent Baathist who was appointed minister of defense, was one of these.

In the period between the Baath Party's accession to power in 1963 and the mid-1970s, the Alawites flourished, as did schools and public facilities in their region. Members of the Alawite community flocked to the universities and became almost the best-educated group in the country. But Hafez al-Assad's accession to power put an end to all this. The tribulations suffered by the minority group to which he belonged had made him fearful and unable to trust anyone outside his own community. It was to this community that he turned in an attempt to safeguard his regime. He encouraged his fellow Alawites to join the army, which, they found, provided them with opportunities for a standard of living they never dreamed of.

Hafez al-Assad's brother Rifaat established a special military unit called the Defense Companies to protect his brother's throne. At the same time another Alawite officer named Ali Haydar set up an additional unit called the Special Forces. Both men concentrated on attracting the rising generation of the Alawite community, using promises of high rank as an incentive. This young generation had found a new area of opportunity that attracted it more than education did, and large numbers of them joined both military units, whose basic function was to protect Hafez al-Assad's throne and regime.

Under Hafez al-Assad the Alawite community, which had been on the verge of becoming the best-educated and most socially aware sector of the Syrian population, began to undergo a process of militarization. As this young generation became militarized, a huge gap opened between the university-educated class, which was fairly well established, and the new, less well educated and less socially aware militarized class. A new struggle broke out between these two classes. Hafez al-Assad began to hunt down members of the educated class and threw large numbers of them in jail.

Once again, this class found itself neglected and oppressed, and those who managed to stay out of prison either left the country or cut themselves off from politics. From his fellow Alawites, Assad expected nothing less than blind obedience and he unsheathed his sharpest weapons against those members of his community who dared to defy him. His fight against them was no less ferocious than his battle with the Muslim Brotherhood, which had been waiting in ambush for him since the first day of his presidency.

When he first came to power, Assad tried to propitiate the Sunni majority so as not to be rejected by it. He attempted to win the support of Sunni clerics and of those with social and economic influence. The mufti* of Syria and other members of the Sunni clergy were among Assad's closest associates and the most vocal champions of his regime. The Muslim Brotherhood was a terrorist movement, and the vast majority of Sunni Muslims rejected it. The Brotherhood, however, took advantage of the truly appalling corruption that had spread into all areas of public life under Assad. The corruption was taking its toll and Assad used it as a trump card to gain favor with the Alawites.

* *Mufti*: a Muslim scholar who interprets the Sharia.

Bribery was rife in government ministries, the standard of living for most Syrians dropped, and wealth became concentrated in the hands of members of the ruling family and a few of its close associates. Though this elite minority included members of a number of different religious communities, most of them were Alawites.

The Baathists, for all their shortcomings, had almost succeeded in smothering the flames of terrorism among the Muslim Brotherhood when the Saudi money that began to shower down upon the organization in the mid-1970s fanned its flames among them once more. I well remember the Baath Party's decision of 1968, when I was in primary school, that performance in religious studies should not determine the future of primary school pupils the way performance in, for example, mathematics or science did. The party could not do away with religious education altogether, but it could reduce its importance, and this was an important step toward withdrawing religious education from the curriculum. No sooner had the Baath Party made this first move to block Islamic expansion than Hafez al-Assad came to power. As a member of a minority he could not take any further similar steps; on the contrary, his fear of the Sunni majority, the womb which had brought forth the Muslim Brotherhood, made him turn a blind eye to the new Saudi-backed Islamic expansion. A bargain was struck: You turn a blind eye to me, and I'll turn one to you.

Corruption ran riot in the ranks of the ruling elite just as Saudi Wahhabism ran riot among the masses of the Sunni populace. Both situations got so out of hand that neither party was any longer capable of considering anything beyond its own interests. While the Syrian president and his entourage were smuggling billions of dollars out of the country and living a life of shameless wealth, most Syrians of all denominations were suffering from degrading poverty.

The Sunnis felt that they had been duped, and welcomed the Muslim Brotherhood—well provided with Saudi money and glutted to the point of indigestion with Islamic teachings—not from a hope that it would improve the situation, but from a desire to be avenged on those responsible for it. The entire Alawite community became the scapegoat, and the educated class, most of whose members Assad had thrown into prison because they had dared to defy him, was easy prey for Islamist terrorism. This class had no way of protecting itself, and the Muslim Brotherhood's secret armed squads hunted down its university-educated members—doctors, engineers, university lecturers, and judges—unmercifully, and murdered them one by one, while Assad's regime stood by and ignored what was happening.

During this period of anarchy I can remember rumors being spread of a deal the Assad family had made with the Saudis, as represented by the Muslim Brotherhood, to the effect that Assad would turn a blind eye to the Brotherhood as long as it did not target Assad or other members of the ruling family personally. Indeed, this is what happened and Syrians followed events as if they were watching a Tom and Jerry cartoon. The struggle became serious only when a detachment of Muslim Brotherhood volunteers attacked a convoy of vehicles in which Assad was traveling, and opened fire on it. They then threw a bomb at the convoy, killing one of Assad's companions, while Assad himself escaped by a miracle.

This 1979 incident caused the whole situation to explode, and the Syrian authorities launched a merciless manhunt. They attacked the Syrian town of Hama, the traditional Muslim Brotherhood stronghold, and pulverized it with tanks, then pursued the defeated remnant in other Syrian cities. This bloody struggle continued for about two years, and many Syrians unconnected with either the authorities or the Brotherhood were among its victims. However, the authorities crushed the Brotherhood only after its failed attempt on the president's life, not in defense of any religious community.

In 1979, when I was in my fifth year of medical school, I witnessed the death of our ophthalmology lecturer, Dr. Yusef al-Yusef. At first I didn't realize who had been killed. The shots that rang out on all sides—sending everyone nearby into a state of shock—mingled with the killer's voice shouting from the loudspeaker: *"Allahu akbar . . . Allahu akbar!"**

Later, when the fear and shock of the attack started to wear off, I discovered that the victim was a man I had looked up to as an ideal of morality and humanity—an upright, generous, and cultured man from a poor family that had sacrificed everything to cover the cost of his medical studies in Europe. He had come back at once and begun his work as a lecturer at the college of medicine. The sound of the killer's voice glorifying God mingled with the sound of the shots. Ever since that moment, Allah has been equated in my mind with the sound of a bullet and become a God who has no respect for human life. From that time on I embarked upon a new journey in a quest for another God—a God who respects human life and values every human being.

---

* When Muslims kill, they shout *"Allahu akbar!"*—"Allah is the greatest!"

Does God exist? As I can perceive his influence, I have to acknowledge his existence. As I have described myself on more
than one occasion as an atheist with no belief in the transcen-
dental, it is only natural that some people regard this insistence
of mine as an incomprehensible contradiction. My response is
this: Though I never saw God throughout my entire life within
the prison of Islam, I did see the influence he wielded, and in
order to dispel his influence I have to deal with him as if he exists. When a young child is afraid of the monster under his bed,
he suffers from the effects of that fear just as he would if the
monster really existed. Things we believe to be real affect us as
if they were real, even if they are no more than an illusion.

God, as I perceive him, arises out of our feeling of need for
him, that need which we cannot satisfy in other ways. God, to
me, is the thing that satisfies that need. People believe in God
in an attempt to fill an intellectual or psychological void that
cannot be satisfied by more realistic methods. He is like a key
fitting into any lock we need to open.

Let me give you an example of what I mean: I was driving
my car down Route 91, bringing my daughter Angela home
from the dentist. Usually the drive home takes half an hour, but
that noonday the roads were jammed with cars and it took us
about an hour to cover half the distance. Angela was due to go
to a friend's birthday party. She got very upset and, as usual,
vented her frustration on me. I suffered her adolescent criticisms
in total silence. Silence is my way of dealing with her fifteen-
year-old adolescent outbursts. Once she had calmed down a bit I
began to chat with her, calmly, so as to avoid another emotional
outburst.

When Angela's emotions were at their height, she opened the car window and said with childish innocence: "I wish I could turn into God right now!" Keeping completely calm I asked her, "And if you did become God, what would you do?" She replied without hesitation, "I would build a special road for myself to take me home now so that I could avoid the traffic jam, get back quickly, and get to my friend's birthday party on time." God, in an attempt to fulfill Angela's need, had become a road-builder!

Of course, sometimes, we ask too much of God. An old woman was standing on the beach watching her adolescent grandson dancing over the surface of the water on his surf-board. After only a few minutes a powerful wave came along and flung him into the depths of the sea. The old woman rushed back and forth until she was exhausted, not knowing what to do. Finally, she dropped to her knees and raised her hands to the heavens: "Lord, oh Lord, bring my grandson safely back to me. I promise not to burden you with demands after this."

No sooner had the grandmother finished uttering her plea than the same wave came along and tossed her grandson safe and sound at her feet. The grandmother knelt and raised her arms to the heavens: "Thank you, Lord, thank you! You've brought my grandson safely back to me, but"—she bowed her head in embarrassment at breaking her promise—"have you forgotten that he was wearing a cap?"

God is our feeling of need for him—a need which extends from the most important request (Lord, bring my grandson back to me safely!) to the most trivial: And don't forget, Oh Most Sublime, that he was wearing a cap!

We ourselves created God, and then we allowed him to create us. We shaped him to fit our need, and then we allowed him to shape us to fit his. We dressed him in our clothes, and then he dressed us in his. With time we got things confused, and we no longer knew which of us had created the other, whether he had created us or we had created him. The question remains: Which came first, the chicken or the egg?

This question is not very important, except when this vicious cycle produces a deformed chicken or a rotten egg. When searching for the reasons for this defect we do not need to know which came first, whether the rotten egg hatched out the deformed chicken or the deformed chicken laid the rotten egg. What I believe is important is that we should begin the job of searching on both levels, and that we should start to re-create both ourself and God at the same time. When we create God then allow him to create us, each of us is responsible for the well-being of the other, and for the degree to which the resulting creation is sound. When one of us is defective, the other is defective, too; and as time passes it becomes hard for us to recognize the point at which the distortion began. If we are serious about rectifying this creational defect we must not waste time answering this question. Instead the time must be used to begin to deal with both axes, both chicken and egg: both God and Man.

In the young man's village I spoke of earlier, just as in my own, people created an ogre that corresponded to the size of their fears, then allowed that ogre to re-create them in his image. After a long time had elapsed, the true facts were lost and no one knew anymore which of them had created the other or which of them was responsible for the other's imperfection. Did the fear which dwelt in the hearts of the inhabitants of the village play a part in the creation of that ogre, or did the ogre implant that terror within them?

The young man was brave. His wanderings and constant traveling had given him a rare degree of courage that helped him to surpass the wisdom of his time, which had warned him against risking his life. Courage is one of the rarest human virtues. To bring about change and rectify defects one must first acquire courage. Wisdom alone cannot change things. On the contrary, sometimes it helps perpetuate a lack of change. Only courage can bring about change. The received wisdom in my village taught me that the eye is no match for the needle, while the courage I acquired after facing the terrors of departure and emigration taught me that my eye can face up to a needle, when that eye is the only weapon I have.

5.

The Nature of God in Islam

BEFORE WE CAN expose the true nature of an ogre, we have to examine the need that produced it, we have to explore, even if only briefly, the environmental circumstances which participated in its creation. When one examines the social, political, and economic situation of the Arabs before Islam that paved the way for its emergence, one can more easily understand the nature of God in Islam.

The people of that era were enveloped in fear, the fear of the unknown. The nature of arid desert life, which made predicting the next moment well nigh impossible, caused people who lived this life to fear what the next moment would bring. Of all human emotions, fear of the unknown is one of the most destructive to one's intellectual and mental capacities. Those who experience this destructive emotion feel an urgent need for security, and are unable to live in the moment, because they are so afraid to face the unknowns they fear.

In the Arabian Desert people did not feel secure for so much as a single day. Raiding was the only way to stay alive and force was the law that governed this means of survival. Consequently, strong tribes raided and plundered their weaker neighbors.

The Arabs became famous for their linguistic knowledge and their ability to express themselves. Anyone who reads the poems, stories, and other works of literature written in that atmosphere charged with the fear of the unknown will realize the extent of that fear and the destructive influence it had on their productivity and creativity. They excelled only in boasting of their courage and daring. But this boasting of theirs was nothing more than a psychological defense mechanism of the kind which evolves in the unconscious to overcome the fear that has taken control of the conscious mind. When a person is fearful he hones his sword, and so the swords of the Arabs were keen, well-honed, and plentiful, both in reality and in their imagination, to the point of taking over every aspect of their lives.

It was in this environment charged with fear that Islam was born. It emerged as a natural response to the psychological need of the people of the Arabian Desert—that need which sought a greater power than that of the fear whose hostage they had become. And so they created an ogre inspired by their fear-ridden imagination, an ogre bigger than their fear, which had the power to enable them to confront everything that frightened them.

They gave this ogre complete power and allowed the ogre to use this to defy all the sources of their fear. They created this ogre, and then allowed it to create them. They grew to resemble it, then internalized it until they merged with it. To protect their ogre, they surrounded it with an iron fence and threatened to slit the throat of anyone who approached it. No one has been able to approach it since, on pain of death.

~◡

Ogres seemed to exist in every story I heard while I was growing up. I remember that when we were young and used to gather around my grandmother every evening, she would often tell us the story of the beautiful young girl who lived alone in a deserted cavern where she was visited every evening by a large ogre that used to bellow outside the cave: "Give me your hand so that I can suck the blood out of it or I'll break it in half!" And the young girl would stretch out her hand through the entrance to the cave and it would suck as much blood as sufficed for its evening meal then leave her, only to come back the next day.

Ever since the day I escaped the clutches of our village ogre I have asked myself why my grandmother was so fond of that story that never seemed to have an ending, the ogre returning every day to prey on the young girl. Perhaps it represented life with my grandfather? Was that beautiful young girl a symbolic representation of my grandmother in the realms of her unconscious?

I can still remember the terror that gripped me when I heard that story. In an attempt to overcome my fears I used to imagine that my father, too, was a big ogre capable of defying the ogre that sucked the hand of the beautiful girl in my grandmother's story. I regarded my father as the only force capable of protecting me, and it was inevitable that I should imagine him as being stronger than the ogre in my grandmother's story, in order to ensure that he would be able to protect me should the ogre come to my room and ask to suck my hand. In my conscious and unconscious mind I had created another ogre, bigger than the one that threatened me, just to guarantee that I would be safe.

The inhabitants of the Arabian Desert could adapt to their fears only by resorting to the same psychological protective mechanism I had used. They proceeded to create an ogre bigger than their fears and capable of vanquishing every source of fear.

The inhabitants of the Arabian Desert bestowed on their new god ninety-nine attributes. Each beautiful attribute was borrowed from the books of the religions that preceded Islam, so as to establish his divine power, while the other attributes were bestowed upon him in order to distinguish him from other gods. His repugnant qualities are not to be found in other gods, while his good qualities were identical with those that preceding gods had displayed.

"The Harmer" is one of the attributes they have given to the God of Islam. Is it reasonable that God should cause harm? Yet this is an attribute which Muslims bestow on their god and take pride in, just as they take pride in describing him as "The Merciful" and "The Patient." "The Subduer," "The Compeller," "The Imperious," "The Humiliator," "The Nourisher," "The Bringer of Death," "The Most High," "The Avenger," "The Protector"—all these are attributes they bestowed upon their ogre and subsequently internalized in an attempt to merge with their ideal.

Whenever I discuss the legitimacy and morality of these names with erudite Muslims I hear nothing but shouts and screams that within minutes turn the dialogue into a futile quarrel. They cannot confront the negativism of these attributes other than by a desperate attempt to justify them, but when they do this they make things worse. Muslims justify portraying God as "The Harmer" because they believe such a portrayal is necessary in order to strike fear into people's hearts and prevent them from disobeying God's commands. They say: "When a person believes in God's ability to harm he will take care not to disobey him, so as to avoid being harmed by him."

I once tried to find common ground on this very point with a Muslim reader from London, an Oxford University graduate with whom I conducted an extensive e-mail correspondence. She wrote to me on one occasion: "Can you deny that God is capable of causing harm? Could he not destroy the universe if he wanted to?" She continued: "What's wrong with proclaiming his destructive powers? Isn't this necessary in order to prevent people from crossing the line and disobeying his commands?"

I replied: "A father has the ability to harm his child when he disobeys him, but does he do so? Is that the proper way to educate our children not to overstep the boundaries we set for them?"

The Oxford graduate responded: "There's no comparison! The difference between God's power and that of a human being is much greater than the difference between a father's and his son's."

I replied: "But shouldn't God's wisdom, mercy, and love far surpass the wisdom, mercy, and love of a father?"

The exchange turned into a fruitless quarrel at the end of which I heard only the e-mailed shouts of the Oxford graduate as she described me as a misguided unbeliever and apostate deserving only of being put to death.

When you teach a child the attributes of God and tell him that he is an avenger, a compeller, imperious, one who subdues, as well as one who nourishes, what have you done to him? You have helped create a vengeful, tyrannical, and overbearing person who also nourishes, but at what cost? For people see their God as their ideal, and strive both consciously and unconsciously to internalize him and merge with him. When we convince them that God is vengeful we justify their becoming vengeful, too. Human nature strives for union with its ideal, so what do you think happens when that ideal is God Himself?

Arguing with Muslims becomes more complicated when they try to persuade you that their God is also merciful, patient, and forbearing. I asked a Muslim doctor who specializes in psychiatry: "How can you persuade your son that God is simultaneously merciful and vengeful? Doesn't teaching this type of religious lesson contain a contradiction which splits the child's personality and makes him feel more lost and confused?"

He replied: "No. I teach him that God is merciful with believers and vengeful toward unbelievers. I don't see any contradiction in this."

I asked again: "How do you teach your son to tell the difference between believers and unbelievers so that he'll know with whom to be merciful and toward whom to be vengeful?"

He said, beaming: "A believer is one who believes in God, his Prophet, and the Day of Judgment and so forth."

I inquired: "So when your son hijacks a civilian plane full of passengers, hurtles into a tower, and kills three thousand 'unbelievers' he won't be doing anything outside the boundaries of what his God and ideal would do? Is that the way to distinguish between believers and unbelievers?"

The conversation ended with shouts and screams and turned into a futile argument that led only to my being accused of blasphemy, apostasy, and sympathy for the enemies of God and his Prophet!

When one lives in an environment beset by the unknown and has difficulty in predicting what the next moment will bring, one is surrounded by fear which eventually results in an inability to act. Islam came into being as a response to this fear. Since people in that environment feared the unknown, Islam fought against probing the depths of anything unknown. Islam dealt with the problem by avoiding the source of the fear, not by preparing to tackle it. The Muslim is a frightened man, and the only way he can deal with his fear is to keep away from what causes it. Everything he distrusts frightens him, and everything he fears he avoids. His education has made him suspicious of everything unfamiliar to him, and this same education has deprived him of his ability to discover the truth about the things he distrusts.

The main source of fear in the environment in which Islam emerged was the unknown. Since every new thing was by definition a variety of the unknown, Islam refused to approach anything new and withdrew into the familiar reality of its own world. Islam, in its teachings, mode of thinking, and way of life, is still captive in a prison whose doors have not opened for fourteen centuries. It is exactly like a man who lives in a hut in the middle of a wood. The hut is Islam and the wood is the unknown. To avoid his fear of the unknown the man has locked all ways in and out of his hut and refuses to go out into the wood. The Muslim treats the world around him in the same way that the man who lives in the hut does. He is afraid of the world around him. His education has not encouraged him to equip himself with the skills necessary for confronting his apprehensions or probing the depths of that world. On the contrary, this education has taught him to fear his surroundings, convinced him to mistrust them, and warned him of the evil that that world holds in store for him.

The relationship between Islam and its adherents on the one hand and the rest of the world, as exemplified by all other religions on the other, is still founded upon fear and mistrust. To a great extent this relationship still resembles and reflects the relationship between the nomadic Bedouin and his desert environment. It is a relationship founded on fear and mistrust. No relationship rooted in fear and mistrust can be sound or healthy, nor can it guarantee the rights of both parties.

In order to safeguard itself from the outside world that threatens its existence and its very being, Islam has made itself inaccessible to the influences of that world. It has surrounded its adherents with an impregnable barrier and locked them inside. It has fought against every innovation, doubting its appropriateness and legality. Its relationship with the world that surrounded it has been characterized by aggression rather than by mutuality and reciprocity. No notable change has taken place inside Islam since the moment it came into being. The only changes that came to Islam came from outside the borders of the authority that the Muslim world has managed to impose on itself.

In the early 1960s, one of the Christian families in our neighborhood bought a television. I remember how the local people talked about them, accusing the head of the family of depravity, and how they planned to pressure them into leaving the neighborhood, fearing for the welfare and morals of their own children and teenagers. The spread of television was very slow, but sure. Today I do not believe that there is a Muslim or Western television program that a Saudi sheikh does not relish watching. And the satellite dishes that transmit the programs from all over the world have stormed the prison Islam created for itself and thoroughly invaded it. The Internet did not encounter the same difficulties as television did, and its invasion was swifter and more influential. Consequently those interested in changing the Islamic world realized that they could use this tool to bring about the abrupt collapse of the impregnable wall surrounding Islam within less than a decade.

In any relationship a Muslim conducts with a non-Muslim, voluntarily or from necessity, the Muslim will remain on the defensive, prepared for the clash with what the unknown elements in this relationship may have in store for him. The Muslim assumes this defensive position because of his fear of the other and his doubts as to the purity of that other's intentions. Such a relationship, no matter how profound it may be or how firmly it may establish itself, can never reach the stage at which it will allow the Muslim to trust the other and like him.

The Muslim will agree to the establishment of such a relationship only in one of two possible situations: to promote his own interests or to harm the interests of the other. When this relationship imposes itself on the Muslim he will display an awesome ability to conceal his feelings. I used to get involved in word battles with some of my expatriate Muslim friends here, especially over their attitude toward Americans and American culture, and would find myself surprised by their terrifying opinions, which revealed enough resentment to destroy not only the towers of the World Trade Center but the whole of America. But should one of my American acquaintances happen along while I was in the company of that same resentful person—in a fraction of second he would become more American than Abraham Lincoln.

I was driving from La Jolla in San Diego to Riverside with my Iraqi friend Amal who had lived in this country for no more than three years. She and her family fled Saddam Hussein's merciless repression of the Shiites in the south and sought refuge in Saudi Arabia, which did not welcome them. They left after America responded to their request for permission to immigrate.

At the entrance to the side road we took on our way to her house a homeless man was standing begging from passersby. My Iraqi friend looked at me and said derisively, "Look at that beggar. That's the America you're so crazy about!"

"My dear, do you really think that's all America has to offer?" I replied.

This was not my first difference of opinion with Amal over our attitudes toward America and its culture. We got into an argument that ended only when we reached her doorstep. I said good-bye to her and left shaking my head, disapproving of every word she had uttered. I have visited a great many different countries but I have never seen a more beautiful stretch of road than that which links La Jolla to Riverside in the state of California, as far as both the natural beauty of the surroundings and skillful planning are concerned. But when my friend Amal looked through the car window at the paradise that surrounded us, she saw only that beggar as representing America.

She deceived others, though, and I always wish that good

Americans could see what I see before it's too late. Amal was an employee of a famous American company. Once, at a party I was invited to, I met the head of the department where she worked, a very cultured and refined American lady. In the course of our long conversation we touched on the topic of emigration and the difficulties emigrants faced when moving to a new country, and I was surprised to hear her say: "What I like about Amal is her love for this country, her great admiration for American values, and her gratitude for what this country has given her." I nodded my head in agreement, while a silent voice inside me murmured: "You poor Americans! If you only realized what Amal thinks of the United States, you'd realize that you're digging your own graves with your naïveté!"

The Muslim's fear of the outside world to a great extent reflects the Bedouin's fear of the desert environment which surrounded him. It was, and still is, a fear of the unknown. In order to triumph over the desert and the unknown he created an ogre larger than his fears in the hope that this ogre would be able to protect him from them, and to offer him a degree of reassurance. But when he created his ogre he was only replacing his existing fear with a greater one.

All Koranic verses that describe paradise portray it as having rivers flowing below it. The desert was very sparing with its water, and death from thirst was one of the greatest dangers of the unknown. The promise of rivers sent a message of reassurance and repose to the Bedouin burdened by fears of death from thirst. The desert had few crops, produced little, and provided almost nothing in the way of food, while Islam promised its followers gardens of date palms, grapes, and other fruit.

Nonetheless, fruit and food are less frequently emphasized than rivers, because fear of death from hunger was less pressing than death from thirst. Paradise in Islam assumed the guise of existing need. It appeared in the form of rivers and fruit to provide reassurance for the Bedouin who feared death from hunger and thirst.

Raiding, which I talked about earlier, was another important source of fear of death and extinction, but at the same time it was the only means of survival. The tribes fought one another in their quest for water and food. The Bedouin did not know a single moment of security. Arab history books are stuffed to bursting with descriptions of raids and of how the tribes would intentionally foment disputes so as to justify their acts of aggression against one another. Raiding was a source of both fear and security. Each tribe was afraid of being raided and felt secure when it got the opportunity to raid someone else.

Being raided meant increased poverty and deprivation for the victim, while for those responsible for the raid it was a source of booty and plunder. Then Islam came and tried to regularize raiding operations, justifying raids by its Prophet and followers, but proscribing raids by others. Open any book about the Prophet Muhammad in Arabic and the first thing you will read about are the Prophet's raiding expeditions. Each of his raids was given a name and described in elaborate detail. The perceptive reader will easily understand that the main objective of these raids was the seizure and division of booty.

Islam tried to justify these raids by regarding them as death in God's cause. Nonetheless, it could not disguise the basic aim, which was, indeed, gain and booty. The Koran mentions booty more than once. It does not forbid it: On the contrary, it entitles the Prophet to take a fifth of it and, so that his followers will not be angry at the size of his share, the name of God is appended to that of the Prophet, and the verse was revealed as follows: "And know that out of all the booty that ye may acquire [in war], a fifth share is assigned to Allah, and to the Messenger, and to near relatives, orphans, the needy, and the wayfarer." (8:41).

In his commentary on the Koran Al-Qurtubi* explains the phrase "and know that out of all the booty ye may acquire" as follows: You took something from the unbelievers by force. This indicates that booty was seized against the will of its rightful owners. Muslim commentators on the Koran could not agree as to how God could take his share of the booty and to whom his share would be given. They simply gave the Prophet the right to dispose of God's share.

Muhammad did not want to leave room for argument with his followers regarding the division of the spoils, and so suggested that these be split five ways, with himself and God receiving one fifth. Had Muhammad suggested that he alone receive a fifth there would have been widespread protest: How could one individual take a fifth of the spoils for himself and leave four fifths for the thousands of others. But when he said "a fifth share is assigned to Allah and to the Messenger," the problem faded, and the others found it hard to arouse dissent. If Almighty and Exalted God had agreed to share his fifth

---

* Al-Qurtubi was a famous classical Muslim scholar (1214–1273). The most famous of his books is *Tafsir al-Qurtubi*, which is a ten-volume commentary on the Koranic verses dealing with Islamic legal issues.

portion with the Prophet, why should the others, however numerous, not be satisfied with the other four fifths?

Here, once again, we see the survival instinct playing a decisive role in the teachings and rulings of Islam, which emerged in an environment dominated by the shadow of the unknown, where death from hunger and thirst posed a constant threat to its inhabitants. Another saying attributed to Muhammad in this connection is: "the killer has the right to his spoils," meaning that when a Muslim kills a non-Muslim, he has the right to despoil him. This *hadith* (Muhammad saying) has caused differences of opinion among Muslims. Some wondered how the killer could be entitled to the spoils when the Koranic verse orders the booty to be divided five ways.

In an attempt to find a compromise between the differing views, some suggested that if there was little to plunder, what little there was belonged to the killer, while if there was a lot, it was divided into five parts. This emphasizes once again the struggle for survival.

In America, when you commit a crime, the first thing the investigators look for is the motive behind the killing. If the victim's wallet and money are found on his body, and if everything in his home is where it should be, the investigators will say, "Basically, theft was not the motive; there would appear to be other motives." But when they establish his possessions are missing, the investigation takes a different turn, as the motives for the murder are different in this case, and it can be surmised that theft is the most important motive behind the killing.

While Muslims justify the Prophet's raids by saying that they were carried out in self-defense, I don't believe that they can justify the theft and the spoils that were gained as a result of this raiding. If someone attacked you suddenly in the dark and tried to kill you and you managed to kill him instead, you could, in such a case, justify your killing him as self-defense. But if you were to steal his wallet and his money after you had killed him, would you be able to justify that by saying: I stole his wallet in self-defense? If you were speaking the truth when you said that you had killed him in self-defense, would you be speaking the truth when you said you had stolen his wallet in self-defense, after you had killed him, too?

The raids Muhammad carried out in his lifetime occupy the major part of his biography. Part two of Ibn Hisham's biography of the Prophet mentions that Muhammad carried out twenty-seven raids in the course of his life, though some Muslim historians report a higher figure. I am not concerned here with following the historical account of these raids. But anyone who has an opportunity to read it from beginning to end will easily be convinced that there can be only two reasons for such raids. The first and most important is the acquisition of booty. The second, necessitated by the first, is to inflict harm upon the tribe that is the victim of the raid.

When the thief ambushes his victim he will be sure, in the course of the crime, to inflict as much damage as possible on him, to ensure that he cannot fight back. Fear of death from hunger and thirst was the main motive for raiding. Causing harm was another objective, and this was done in order to guarantee that the raider's enemy had been deprived of his ability to resist. Islam legalized it, legitimized it, and justified it with an edict from the ogre it had created in order to overcome its fear of the environment that threatened its survival and its very existence.

For me, understanding the truth about the thought and be-havior of Muslims can only be achieved through an in-depth understanding of this philosophy of raiding that has rooted it-self firmly in the Muslim mind. Bedouins feared raiding on the one hand, and relied on it as a means of livelihood on the other. Then Islam came along and canonized it. Muslims in the twenty-first century still fear they may be raided by others and live every second of their lives preparing to raid someone else. The philosophy of raiding rules their lives, the way they be-have, their relationships, and their decisions.

When I immigrated to America I discovered right away that the local inhabitants were not proficient in raiding while the expatri-ate Muslims could not give it up. After I had been in the United States for only a few weeks, an Arab neighbor of mine took me to the supermarket in an attempt to familiarize me with the area we lived in. We went into a Vons market and, once there, she began to open every packet she could, then she began to make holes in the lids of cartons of milk, Jell-O, and cream. Then she made holes in a number of bags of potato chips, packets of paper handkerchiefs, and packets of spaghetti.

I shouted at her disapprovingly: "Dina, what are you do-ing?"

"May God curse them. They stole our land!"

"And are you doing this to try to get it back?"

"I'm trying to hurt them! You're still new here. Don't you know the owner's Jewish?"

That happened over fifteen years ago when I was a new-comer here. But today I am more firmly convinced than ever that time can do nothing to change this mentality, and that the less able a Muslim feels to adapt to his surroundings the more he feels the need to go raiding. He is convinced that he has come to this country to despoil it and cause harm.

The municipality of the town where I live in California gives each household three garbage cans: one for nonrecyclable refuse; one for glass, paper, and metal recyclables; and a third for garden refuse. I was once invited to a luncheon party at the home of a Muslim woman friend. When the party was over we began to clear the table and she started to collect the refuse and throw it in the garbage can. I asked her in surprise, "Don't you sort the rubbish into its different cans?" She replied angrily, "God curse them! Do you expect me to help them look after their environment? Don't you know what they did in the first and second Gulf War? They poisoned our country's environment with their waste. Have you heard about the prostitutes with AIDS whom Israel sends to Jordan and Egypt so as to spread AIDS in our countries?"

In an attempt to silence this recital, which I was weary of hearing, I said, "Yes, I have."

My friend knows that she will live her whole life in this country, she knows that this will be the home of her children, her grandchildren, and her grandchildren's grandchildren. Yet she seems to care nothing for the state of its environment, for she is here only to pillage and cause harm to her enemies. The idea or philosophy of raiding has taken root in her mind as well and was a motivating factor in her immigration to this country. She regards the comforts here as her own private booty and her actions, to me, seem to be just one more Muslim attempt to harm others.

~

Muslims eat raiding, dress raiding, talk raiding, and drive their cars like raiders. To see the truth of what I am saying you have only to observe a Muslim preaching a sermon on a Friday in any mosque anywhere in the Muslim world. You don't need to understand the language he is preaching in: you have only to listen to his shouts and observe his gestures in order to become acquainted with the art of raiding. I was born and brought up in a small town that contains four mosques—one in each quarter—where public prayers are performed on Fridays.

On Fridays all activity in the town stopped. The men retired to the mosques for prayers while the women remained shut up at home with their children and eavesdropped on the sermon from windows and balconies. There was no concord between voices from the various mosques. Each preacher gave voice stridently and their shouts were deafening. Our home was very close to one of these mosques, so close that it felt as if the mosque's loudspeaker were in the bedroom. Our family, like everyone else, had to put up with this noise pollution.

When I look back and remember those days I know that I began, at a very early age, to refuse to allow anyone to raid my world without my permission. The voice of the muezzin burst into my bedroom at five o'clock in the morning and I struggled with myself, even at a young age, as to how I should respond. Why was I irritated by this early-morning raid? It was bringing me the voice of God and his Prophet. Why would I reject the voice of God and his Prophet? Surely God is severe in retribution! I rejected the shouting, but, at the same time, I was afraid to reject it.

My confusion was compounded by my mother's reaction to the shouting. My mother is illiterate. She can barely read or write a single word. Arabic is different from many other languages in that the official language used for reading and writing is completely different from the colloquial language used in conversation. Illiterate people are perfectly fluent in the colloquial language, but are virtually unable to comprehend the form of Arabic used for reading and writing. My mother had never read the Koran or any other book on Islam, its teachings or its history. Her knowledge did not extend beyond what was transmitted orally by the local women from one generation to the next. Naturally, my mother could not understand what the preacher in the mosque was saying. Although she could perhaps pick out a word here and there, she most certainly could not understand any of the expressions used. Nonetheless, listening to the preacher at the local mosque fascinated her. She would rate preachers by the stridency and volume of their voices and the degree of emotion they displayed; some she praised, with others she found fault.

My mother was fascinated by the shouting and I hated it. I had to work this out for myself and I have parted company with the culture of shouting and raiding in the Islamic environment. My experience has been that two Muslims cannot talk together without their conversation turning into shouts within minutes, especially when they disagree with each other, and no good can come of that. When you talk to a Muslim, rationally, in a low calm voice, he has trouble understanding your point of view. He thinks you have lost the argument. A Muslim conversing with anyone else—Muslim or non-Muslim—cannot remember a single word the other person has said, any more than my mother could remember a single word of what the preacher in our local mosque said.

6.

Muslim Men and Their Women

FEAR, OF COURSE, extends in the Muslim world to the way men treat their women. It is, in many ways, the vilest and most hateful treatment the Muslim world visits on others.

I was in my fourth year at medical school. A woman came to the gynecological clinic at the university hospital where I was doing my training and complained of a number of symptoms. When the doctor examined her he found a number of inflamed circular burns the size of small coins on her thighs and abdomen. The doctor on duty that day, who was head of the hospital's gynecological department, asked her: "What's this?"

She hid her head in her hands with embarrassment and replied in a voice that was barely audible: "My husband stubs out his cigarettes on my body to punish me for being a stupid woman."

Without pausing to think even for a moment Dr. Saad replied: "You must deserve it. He wouldn't do it if you weren't really stupid." The students laughed and I laughed openly with them to gratify the vanity of our teacher, whom we wanted to please.

Dr. Saad had studied medicine in Britain and would often

tell us of the shameless conduct of the godless British women. He saw nothing in Britain except shamelessness, and he forgot that it was there that he had learned of a doctor's moral and legal responsibility toward a woman who had been subjected to abuse.

The telephone rang in the emergency room of the hospital where I worked. I lifted the receiver and was surprised to hear a voice raging at the other end: "This is Dr. Ahmad. I'm sending you a whore. Open up her cunt and take out what you find in there!" He hung up without giving me the chance to ask for an explanation. A cold shudder ran through my body and I felt I might faint. Addressing a woman in street language of that kind shows profound contempt for her womanhood, her dignity, and her humanity, especially if she is a doctor and the speaker is her colleague.

Dr. Ahmad was head of the town's medical administration and a large number of patients attended his private clinic and paid him higher fees than any other doctor could command, not because they had faith in his medical abilities, but because they had faith in his prestige, which enabled him to get them free treatment at this state-run hospital.

Suha, the young girl Dr. Ahmad called "a whore," arrived in the emergency room about half an hour after this telephone conversation. She was a thin pale girl of under twenty dressed in rags insufficient to keep out the cold of that icy February day. As she walked over to the examination table she waddled like a sick duck on the verge of departing this life. The vaginal examination revealed a medium-sized conical glass inside her.

"What's this, Suha?"

She buried her face in her hands and burst into copious tears: "One of them shoved it up my vagina."

"What do you mean by 'one of them'?"

"Mr. X. I clean his office and he pays me a monthly wage, which I use to help my unemployed father bring up my seven sisters."

"But why did he do it?"

"He said I was dirty and that his sperm was too sacred to touch my body."

"And what do you think?"

Her voice was hoarse with crying. "I think I am dirtier than dirt," she said.

When I was working in one of the rural areas, Fatima, a peasant woman in her late thirties, came to our clinic complaining of nausea, vomiting, and back pain. An examination revealed that her womb was of a size which indicated the third month of pregnancy. As soon as I told her the news she collapsed on the chair opposite and began to shudder, smack her own face, and shriek, "I beg you, Doctor, I beg you to rescue me from the mess I'm in. My son will kill me. I don't care about my life. I deserve to die, but I don't want my son to dirty his hands with my blood."

"What is it, Fatima?"

"I'm a widow. My husband died five years ago and left me with four children. My husband's brother rapes me every day in exchange for feeding my children. If he knew I was pregnant he'd provoke my son into killing me rather than be exposed to public disgrace."

"How old is your son?"

"He's fifteen. Doctor, I'm begging you! He's still young and I don't want him dirtying his hands with my filthy blood!"

I sent her to see a gynecologist. When she came back to see me about two weeks later, she looked gaunt, haggard, and ill.

"What is it, Fatima?"

"I came to thank you. I got rid of the fetus, but I saw the angel of death with my own eyes! They performed the operation to remove the fetus without an anesthetic, and the pain of it nearly killed me."

"He did it without an anesthetic! Why?"

"I didn't have enough money to pay for the drugs to anesthetize me, so the doctor had to operate without them."

Amal—a different Amal than the one who had such disregard for America—was a doctor who worked at the same hospital as I did. One day I heard that she had been rushed urgently to the eye department the previous night after suffering chemical burns to the face and eyes. I went to her room at once and asked, "What happened, Amal, my dear?"

"I slipped in the bathroom while I was trying to light the water heater, the pail of fuel fell on my head, and I suffered some burns."

Days passed, and once I was alone with Amal and we were able to have a private talk, she told me what really happened. "That evening I was about to leave the house to go to a friend's wedding. My brother, who is fifteen years younger than me and never graduated from high school, came up to me and warned me not to leave the house. When I tried to push him away he took the fuel bucket and poured it over my head. I'm almost forty, Wafa, and I still dream of a husband who will rescue me from life with my brother and father." Then she continued, "But what guarantee do I have that my future husband will be any better than them. It's a trap, and it's very hard indeed to get out of it. And just imagine what my mother said to me when I talked to her about it. 'You got what you deserved! I've warned you more than once not to go against your brother's wishes, and now you've paid the price for your stubbornness.' Wafa, I sometimes think that it's not just men who are against women, but women themselves who are hostile to other women. All my scientific and educational accomplishments are not enough to give me the credibility to run my own life, and my brother, who doesn't know how to write his own name, is considered better equipped to look after me than I am myself."

Aleppo was the Muslim Brotherhood's most important stronghold after Hama, and they committed a great many crimes there. I found life there unbearable and decided to move to a teaching hospital attached to a different university in another town, and so Lattakia became my next stop. Lattakia is a tranquil town slumbering on the shores of the Mediterranean north of Baniyas, where I was born and grew up.

At the time Lattakia had two training hospitals. I applied to the smaller and less crowded of the two—a military hospital that treated Syrian army personnel and their families—and was accepted at once.

My decision to leave Aleppo brought Morad to the brink of emotional collapse. He had become used to spending most of his time with me, far from his problems with society and his mother, and was convinced that our relationship would suffer if I went away. He had graduated from university two years earlier but was not working in the field in which he had specialized. He wanted to stay close to me and, in order to do so, had accepted a humble post on the university campus.

My mother had visited me a number of times in Aleppo, where she had stayed with Ahmad and Huda, and I had had no choice but to introduce her to Morad so that she would not be shocked by any rumors she might hear from them. She liked Morad from the very first but had concealed her feelings from me in order to avoid any appearance of legitimizing our relationship. She alternated between encouraging me to keep seeing him, so as to ensure that we would marry, and refusing to acknowledge a relationship that overstepped the bounds of convention, so as not to have to take responsibility for having sanctioned it. No woman in our society, even if she were a mother, could assume responsibility for such a thing, and she would tell me from time to time, "Just you wait and see what your brother has to say!"

My decision to leave Aleppo almost put an end to my relationship with Morad. He appeared to be on the verge of a breakdown, and I had no choice but to let him meet my brother and tell him he wanted to marry me. We decided things on the spur of the moment, without any preparation. He didn't even have enough money to buy me a wedding ring, let alone enough money to raise a family. Deep in my heart, I knew what my brother's reaction would be. The person who had treated me with respect from the moment my father had died would not be a stumbling block on my path to happiness. Morad called my brother and introduced himself, then asked if he could go and visit him, and my brother welcomed the idea.

Morad sat down to lunch with my brother and his family in

accordance with the Syrian custom that decrees that the guest must lunch at the host's home on the first visit, especially if that guest has just arrived after a long journey. Morad was twenty-seven years old at the time. Cultured, sensitive, and quietly spoken, he avoided looking other people directly in the face. However, he rose to the occasion and was sufficiently composed to explain our relationship to my brother—without going into too much detail—and to express his hopes of obtaining his consent to our marriage. My brother's warm welcome and willingness to listen helped to reduce the tension of the occasion, and he told Morad as they shook hands on parting, "It was a pleasure to meet you. Give me a little time to ask my sister what she thinks, as the decision is hers, not mine. I wish you good luck!"

Never, as long as I live will I forget my first meeting with my brother after he had met Morad. It was, without doubt, the most difficult moment of my life. He asked me what I knew about Morad and if I in all conscience and understanding wanted to marry him. He tried to explain to me that, though he would raise no objections under any circumstances, he wanted me to be judicious in my decision and not to be in any hurry, as I was still young and had another year of studies ahead of me before I graduated. I summoned all my strength and told my brother of my admiration for this young man, explaining that I had met him at university and had come to realize through our meetings that he would be a suitable life partner for me.

My brother gave my decision his blessing and telephoned Morad to congratulate him. I borrowed some money from my sister, who was a year older than me, had already graduated from university, and now had a good job. I used the money to buy two rings for Morad and myself, but asked him to keep quiet about this and not to let anyone know that my sister had paid for them. Morad returned to our house with the sheikh and the two rings, which he pretended to have bought himself. The engagement ceremony was conducted quietly, in accordance with Muslim teaching, which, though it supports public celebration of marriage, insists upon discreet engagements for one reason: If the couple changes their minds, the girl might miss her chance to marry someone else since most men would rather not marry a girl who has already been engaged to another suitor.

We got engaged in August and decided to get married that same month. My brother was not very happy with our decision, which he considered rash. People firmly believed that it was unlucky to get married in the two months and ten days between the end of Ramadan and the Feast of the Sacrifice. My brother took advantage of this and suggested postponing the marriage, hoping that I would change my mind in the intervening period, but I insisted on getting married immediately after the Feast of the Sacrifice. We rented a small furnished apartment near the hospital I had moved to in Lattakia. On October 10, at a small party for friends and family, we said our good-byes and left Baniyas for a new life.

My husband exchanged his job at Aleppo University for one at the University of Lattakia, where he earned enough to pay our rent and buy a few basic necessities. I supplemented this with occasional help from my family. Immediately after our marriage, I discovered I was pregnant and thought that I would lose my mind. We both now faced a new problem that depended on our capacity to assume parental responsibilities.

I decided to have an abortion, but my mother intervened at once and declared that such a thing would be done only over her dead body and I had no choice but to go ahead with the pregnancy. Syrian society allows its members no privacy, and decisions cannot be taken in isolation; the opinions of both family and society have to be taken into consideration.

In any case, my marriage provided me with a partial release from family and social pressures. In Islam, a husband owns his wife just as he does the furnishings of his home. My mother was well aware of this, and in order to assert her authority, she took advantage of the fact that we needed financial help from the family, and she triumphed. I am glad that she did, as our son, Mazen, was the result of that pregnancy. I gave birth to Mazen on the first day of the Muslim festival that marks the end of the monthlong Ramadan fast, on August 1, 1981. Fate decreed that my brother should come to visit me that same day, only to be told that I was in the hospital, where the doctors had decided to perform a cesarean as I was having a very difficult birth.

On the way from the operating theater to my room, while I was still under the influence of the anesthetic, he came over to where I was lying and planted a kiss on my forehead, saying jokingly, "Don't be upset that you've had to have an operation. You've got a son, and he's as handsome as his maternal uncle."

I did not get a chance to talk to him before he left the hospital, as he had to catch the bus from Lattakia back to Baniyas before the bus station closed. After he left the hospital that day, I never saw him again. It is one of fate's ironies to give with one hand and take away with the other. Fate gave me Mazen and took Muhammad from me in the space of a single day. My brother died from a heart attack ten minutes after he got home. He was forty-four years old.

Muhammad's death shocked and saddened me, but at the same time released me to a certain extent from my familial and social obligations. He was the only person I had loved and respected, and for his sake I had felt obliged to submit to many social conventions in order to preserve our relationship. After his death there was no one else whose opinion I cared about. Even after my marriage I felt I had to do everything I could to please my brother, even if he did not directly tell me to do so. I knew what he wanted and what he did not, and did my best to please him. After my marriage and his death I became relatively free of obligations. I set no great store by the opinion of my other brothers, especially as I was now married, and, in the eyes of Islam, the exclusive property of my husband.

I had now spent five years away from my family and close to Morad. This had allowed me to begin to think for myself, and my personality was now formed to a certain extent. After our marriage, my domestic life with Morad was very different from our life outside the home. Together, protected from the influence of our surroundings, we tried to construct a belief system different from that of most other people, and we kept ourselves to ourselves.

I was an avid reader, fascinated by anything that could tell me about life in the West, beyond the confines of the ideological prison we lived in. My sister had a friend who worked at the public library. Through her I was able to borrow a number of books, and for long time I was in the habit of photocopying articles. A neighbor of ours, who was originally from Lebanon, would smuggle in many of the books I wanted when he returned from his frequent visits to his homeland. In exchange, I provided free medical treatment for him and his family.

On one occasion he brought me two books by a Saudi writer and thinker named Abdullah al-Qasimi whose life had been declared forfeit in Saudi Arabia. He fled to the West, and no one knows what has become of him since. Two of his books, "The World Is Not a Mind" and "This Universe—What Is Its Conscience?," gave me an intellectual shock when I read them. Their contents turned my whole life upside down. My husband and I began to hold daily discussions on various aspects of Al-Qasimi's thought, every detail of which we had begun to adopt. We did not dare tell anyone what we were reading lest we should be accused of apostasy. My husband was more receptive to what he read than I was. Like most Muslims today, I tried to interpret everything on the basis of a belief that I was frightened to see contradicted: I believed that people's interpretation of Islam, rather than Islam itself, was responsible for the shortcomings of our Muslim countries. My husband did not agree with me on this point, but this difference of opinion between us was not so serious as to affect the warm friendship that bound us, and each of us continued to respect the other's opinions.

My husband had felt from the outset that my belief that it was Muslims rather than Islam that was at fault would perhaps help to protect us from the potentially serious consequences of living in a society that did not permit its individual members to take the smallest step toward examining any of its taboos, and so he did not object to my thinking as I did. When we got into discussions with people at social events I would assume the role of faithful sentinel, keeping a close watch over everything Morad said, and intervening and reinterpreting his remarks in a more acceptable manner whenever it looked as if he might be straying into dangerous territory. Because I was very careful never to come close to crossing the line myself, Morad felt secure because he knew I was there to protect him whenever he felt the need to get things off his chest. His childhood and the circumstances of his life seemed to make it easer for him to believe that the fault lay in Islam itself, and that Muslims were victims of their belief system.

During the first five years of my marriage I moved gradually to a different stage in my thinking in which I allowed myself to ask questions about the truth of our Muslim beliefs and culture, and started looking for answers. We passed around books in secret, as if they were opium. Al-Qasimi denied the existence of God and attacked Islam, analyzing it in such as way as to make the most closed mind stop and really think. He was an original and creative writer with an excellent command of Arabic. His style was enjoyable to read and easy to understand, and it led his readers almost imperceptibly to the point where they could not help but agree with him, at least privately. The fact that he was from Saudi Arabia, the cradle of Islam, gave him another kind of authenticity. His books were not readily available, but we found a way to get copies and share them. I remember a young woman in her early twenties at the hospital where I worked once confessed to me secretly that she read Al-Qasimi's works, and asked if she could borrow one of them from me. I wrapped the book in one of my dresses to conceal it and, as I gave it to her, made a great show of telling her she could wear the dress to her sister's wedding on condition she return it afterward.

The Egyptian doctor Nawal el-Saadawi also played an important role in my intellectual reprogramming. Although her books were not as strictly forbidden as Al-Qasimi's, her ideas were anathema to most sections of society. She became my mentor, and her books gave me a glimmer of hope for a future that nothing else in our society indicated would be any better than the present. After I had finished reading her book *The Female Is the Source,* I felt as if I had been revived from a drug-induced coma. In a society that believes the Prophet Muhammad's dictum that a man's prayer is nullified if a dog or a woman passes close beside him, it is not easy for a writer to say that the female is the source.

Dr. El-Saadawi lived in the same society as I did—a society that does not just believe that women are dirty, but considers anyone who does not believe this an infidel, and calls for him to be killed. In a society such as that it was not easy for Dr. El-Saadawi to prove her contention, nor was it easy for women like me to adopt her ideas. Dr. El-Saadawi is still an ideal figure and an example as far as I am concerned, and I acknowledge that she played a major role in making me the person I am today.

In 1984 my husband was a member of a Syrian delegation that was sent to Britain to study teaching methods. At the time he was a lecturer at the Faculty of Agriculture at Syria's Tishreen University. His trip was another turning point in our lives, as he was now able to observe in practice in the West the things we had learned from books. He was astonished by British society, just as a prisoner born behind bars is astonished the first time he experiences life on the other side of them.

He sent me a secret message telling me: "Take Mazen and go to the British Embassy then just leave everything and get out! Life here's different but I can't go into details." Naturally, I refused to do anything of the kind. I knew that he was in England at the expense of the Syrian government, that his visa would run out as soon as the allotted time was up, and that he had no skills to help him build a new life. He remained in Britain for three months, then came back home at my request. His experiences in Britain continued to preoccupy him, however, and he talked about them from the day he came home until the moment he left for the United States four years later.

His three-month stay in Britain confirmed his deep-rooted conviction that we in our Muslim societies were slaves to a doctrine that neither respected people nor valued their ideas. For some reason I continued to disagree with him about this, and insisted that the problem lay with Islam's followers, not in Islam itself. When I look back now and try to understand my insistence on this point, I can find no convincing reason for me to cling to this point of view other than the survival instinct, which made me adopt this attitude to protect our safety and our lives.

Without our being aware of it, our new beliefs began to affect the way we lived. We no longer practiced any form of religious observance and avoided visiting my family during the month of fasting. Moreover, our attitudes affected the way we treated each other. Most of our acquaintances accused me of being a domineering woman and my husband of being weak. When a man treats his wife with respect and listens to her opinions, he is thought weak and she is considered bossy. Whenever my mother came to stay with us she would express indignation at the way I treated my husband if, for example, I asked him to bring me a glass of water while we were sitting at the dinner table. She was accustomed to a tradition in which a woman waited upon her husband, and in which it was unseemly for her to ask him to do anything for her. I would argue with my mother, and she would usually leave the house swearing never to visit us again.

My two brothers were no less critical of the way my husband and I behaved and, half jokingly, half seriously, would refer to my husband as my slave. My husband treated their jokes with magnanimity and insisted that I was a woman who deserved to be treated well. Our "odd" beliefs—as others considered them—set us apart, and we were sometimes accused of being Marxists, as people believed that anyone who deviated from Islam had to be a godless communist.

I graduated from medical school in 1981, three months after Mazen was born, and was immediately given a job as a doctor in a mountain village far from the center of the country and sixty kilometers away from the nearest first-aid center. My husband and I moved to the village called "Kinsebba" and rented a house from the local sheikh, Muhammad. He looked after the mosque, called people to prayer at the appointed times, and lived in a little room behind our house.

The sheikh's wife and seven children lived far away in another town where some of them were at university, and came to visit him only for a short period over the summer holidays, as they were not on good terms with him. We became very friendly with the sheikh, largely because he was a cheerful man with a sense of humor, and we would spend long hours together in half-serious, half-humorous discussion of Islam and its teachings. He often repeated to us his dictum: "Believe me, if they stopped paying mosque sheikhs' salaries, there wouldn't be a single mosque left open in all Syria!" I remember one stormy winter's day when the village was struck by lightning and the sheikh discovered the following morning that the minaret and its equipment had been damaged. He came back to us smiling, saying jokingly, "I thank God for having given me a holiday until the mosque gets repaired."

He treated my husband and me as if we were his children, trusting and confiding in us. He told us more than once of his experiences as a policeman and how he would accept bribes and beat people up in the interrogation rooms. Later he changed jobs and became a truck driver, and he told us how he would steal some of the goods he was transporting. Later still he became a doorkeeper at a brothel, before eventually returning to his native village after his wife and children had disowned him. He repented, asked God for forgiveness, and became the village sheikh. His fondness for joking was not in any way frivolous; rather, it reflected the psychological struggle he was engaged in, which I had observed ever since we had first met him.

Our friendship with him increased our doubts regarding the sincerity of the clergy, and in our conversations with him we often strayed into forbidden territory on the pretext of just joking around. He was by no means an ignorant man and was a fine practitioner of the art of conversation. He may have sensed from the outset that we wanted to use the appearance of joking to arrive at a number of truths. He himself had never doubted the truth of Islamic teachings for a minute. Nonetheless, he would usually evade answering direct questions by saying that only God knew, leaving us with the impression that he himself was not fully convinced of what he believed. In this he was very different from other sheikhs, who insisted that they had a monopoly of absolute truth.

When we left the village after three years of living next door to him, we had hundreds of unanswered questions. Our friendship with him had intensified both our doubts and our desire to search for the truth. However, I still insisted on retaining my links with Islam, fragile as they were.

Sheikh Muhammad was not our only local source of doubts regarding the teachings of Islam. During my time in the village I faced challenges of another kind. Its primitive rural society did not acknowledge that a woman was capable of being a doctor. In our first year there, I managed, through patience and persistence, to win the trust of the villagers, and of the women in particular. At night our house turned into an emergency room. I would be awakened in the middle of the night by knocking at the door and the sound of a voice calling out, "Please, Dr. Morad, open the door, we need Wafa." My husband is not a doctor but the villagers called him "doctor" nonetheless, while addressing me by my first name.

Because they trusted me, I penetrated further into their homes than even the rays of the sun did, and experienced first-hand all the secrets that lay behind their locked doors. What I found there appalled me and made me want to protest; but my voice was stifled by my fear for our own lives, which prevented me from speaking out against the injustices I witnessed.

The month of Ramadan, during which Muslims neither eat nor drink from sunrise to sunset, was one of the hardest months of the year for me. Many more patients flocked for treatment at the medical center where I worked than the number we usually saw. The number who collapsed from exhaustion and dehydration soared startlingly during the day, as did the number of those who suffered from indigestion and vomiting at night, as they stuffed themselves with food in an attempt to compensate for their daytime fast. Both men and women worked in the fields from early morning, performing arduous and exhausting agricultural labor, which, especially when the weather was hot, necessitated large quantities of water that the fast did not allow them to drink. Spurred on by my feelings of pity for them, I tried to persuade them—the women, especially—not to fast, then withdrew my suggestion when it was met with disdainful glances.

It goes without saying that the men treated their women inhumanely and, in this rural society, they were even more pitifully exploited. Many of them gave birth in the open fields, and I would sometimes be called out to help a woman whose labor pains had come upon her as she tilled the ground. My anger rose as I stood helpless, not knowing what to do in the face of such injustice. Sometimes I would exert my authority as a doctor and scream at the men, "Don't you feel guilty at all?," but they would usually just laugh and refuse to take my question seriously.

The exploitation of women as a workforce was not, however, my main concern. I was much more worried by the sexual abuse they suffered. Because I was a woman, I got to know about a great many cases that a male doctor would never have learned of. Although sexual assault was widespread in the area, it was well protected from the view of others. By showing my sympathy for the women I was able to win their confidence, and they told me secrets of a kind they usually took to the grave. Many had been raped and most of these rape victims had fallen prey to male members of their own family, usually their own fathers. Unmarried women who became pregnant as a result of these rapes were murdered as soon as their condition was discovered to wash away the disgrace and keep the scandal hidden. In some cases the murderer was the rapist himself. Some victims were deliberately poisoned with the pesticides that were used to spray the apple trees in that region famous for its apple production. The death certificate would read: "Death from natural causes." No doctor was required to obtain a death certificate for these women. Witnesses were sufficient.

By the time I had completed my period of service in the village my heart had bled and I was seething with fury. I returned to Lattakia three years later a more experienced woman, well schooled in the human rights abuses that took place in the society in which I lived.

7.

First Step to Freedom

AT THE END of the 1980s the world accused Syria of supporting world terrorism; its name was added to the international terrorism list and rigorous economic sanctions were imposed on it. I believe it was at about this time that a young Palestinian who held a Syrian passport placed a bomb in his girlfriend's suitcase before she boarded a plane at a London airport. After his action was discovered the culprit took refuge in the Syrian Embassy in London, and British police had to storm the building before they could arrest him. After this incident Syria broke off diplomatic ties with Britain, and its relations with the international community reached a crisis point.

The economic sanctions began to affect Syria, and life there in the last four years of the 1980s became an unbearable hell. The ideological oppression rife in Syrian Muslim society on the one hand and its dictatorial regime on the other made young Syrians want to look for somewhere else in the world to live. Then the deteriorating economic situation poured oil on the flames and made them feel even more unjustly treated, further increasing their desire to emigrate.

My husband spent many nights waiting outside every single

foreign embassy in Damascus, and we suffered repeated disappointments each time another embassy turned down our application. He spent most of our income on fares for his journeys back and forth to Damascus, where all the foreign embassies were, and on the hotels where he stayed while he waited to submit his papers to yet another consulate. I became impatient with his constant traveling and his unceasing search for somewhere else to live, as they were eating up most of our income. But whenever I brought the issue up he would tell me hopefully, "I'm utterly convinced I don't belong in this country and that there is somewhere else in the world that deserves me more."

In May 1988 the miracle came to pass and confirmed that my husband had been right in thinking that there was another country waiting for him that deserved him more than the land of his birth did. He received his visa for the United States, and left Syria eight months before I did. During the period we were separated he wrote to me at least twice a week. In his letters he described to me at length and in detail his impressions of American society. I still have those letters. In one of them he wrote, "Today I saw an American woman climbing an electricity pole to carry out some repairs—can you believe it?" In another letter he told me, "I saw on TV today how American emergency services tried to rescue a little cat that had fallen into a pit. Their attempts continued for about two hours, and everyone clapped when the cat was brought out alive."

When I read his letters to my colleagues at the hospital where I worked I was accused of being dazzled by American society and ignoring its moral decadence. Privately I sometimes wondered what our conception of morality was, and why we should not consider an action like the American emergency services' rescue of a kitten to be a moral act. I wondered, why are people in our homeland less well treated than a cat in America? I couldn't understand why my colleagues considered the United States to be a morally decadent society when they had no firsthand knowledge about it. If the United States is morally decadent, I wondered, then why are so many of my fellow Syrians standing in line at the door to its embassy? I knew that the only way I could answer all these questions was to join my husband and write about it firsthand.

My husband knew that I had a gift for writing and an unusually fine command of literary Arabic, and insisted in his letters to me that life in the United States would give me a unique opportunity to attain prominence as a writer in the Arab world. The dream of leaving grew day by day, and the way the people around me gossiped about my husband's absence made me cling to it all the more and increased my longing to escape from a society in which I could not reconcile my religious convictions with the reality I observed around me.

On December 15, 1988 I got a heaven-sent gift: I received my American visa, after spending three days and nights outside the U.S. consulate in Damascus. Waiting before me in line was a Muslim woman, veiled from head to toe, who constantly repeated verses from the Koran and implored God to help her get her visa. She turned to me and said, "Daughter, repeat this prayer and I'm sure your wish will be granted: Say 'God is one, Oh Lord, blind their hearts and their sight.'" I looked at her in surprise and asked, "Why do you want God to blind their hearts and their sight?" She replied, "Because if they knew the truth they'd never give me a visa. My husband's in America already and we're planning to stay there."

I lifted my face to the heavens and pleaded, "Oh Lord, set me on the path to freedom and I promise You that I will fight for the freedom of others."

On the twenty-fifth of that same month, on Christmas night, the plane set me down in Los Angeles, where my husband was waiting to greet me. He was living in a small apartment, and his next-door neighbor was an American lady. When she heard that he was going to the airport to meet me she hoisted an American flag at the door of her apartment and told him: "Tell your wife that America welcomes her."

I was overwhelmed with happiness when I saw the flag and realized why my husband's American neighbor, Diane, was flying it. She was unable to pronounce my Arabic name and so decided to give me an American one: She began to call me "Pam." I did not like the name very much for the simple reason that in Arabic we do not have the sound *p*, and so, when we try to say it, we pronounce it like a *b*. It made Diane laugh to hear me introduce myself to others as *Bam*. Bam was the first word I looked up in the English dictionary, and when I learned it is used to indicate a sudden impact, I ran over to Diane's to suggest changing the name. I told her, "Diane, I'd rather be called Lina than Bam." She laughed, and today she still calls me Lina. When I recall this episode now, I wonder if it was mere chance that. I had accidentally referred to myself as Bam—or was it my fate?

That same week I registered at California State University's, Long Beach, language institute. There were about fifteen students in the class—myself, a woman from El Salvador, a man from Yemen—and the rest were all Japanese. I was like a child entranced by a new toy. I had never met anyone from El Salvador or Japan before, or even anyone from Yemen, an Arab country only two hours away from Syria by plane, and I was glad to make the acquaintance of all of them. In my limited broken English I was able to learn from them within a short time things I had never learned in my own country.

My English was confined mainly to the medical terms I had learned while studying to become a doctor, but nonetheless, from the very start, I felt a great desire to acquire the language. I recall that on one occasion the teacher asked each of us to read a page in the *Los Angeles Times* and talk about it. I spent a long time leafing through the paper looking for an article that would be easy to read and prepare. My search led me to the Calendar section where I found what I was looking for: the "Dear Abby" column. The first time I read it, I became an addict. Getting to know "Abby" through her column proved to be another important turning point in my life. "Abby" receives letters from readers with problems, to which she proposes a solution. People may laugh when I say this, but you can learn a lot about America by reading "Dear Abby." Through the people who wrote to her with their myriad of problems, I began to learn about the greater social issues in the United States, both the good and the bad. In turn, reading these letters, even filled with problems as they were, revealed to me the advantages of life in America and, very slowly, made me fall in love with it.

I believe that the quickest way to learn about a society's advantages is to learn first of all about its problems and how it deals with them. Every time I read about a reader's problem and the solution she proposed I would imagine the type of solution Islam might suggest and be frustrated at the difference between the two. I would wonder how many Dear Abbys our Muslim world would need in order to solve our problems in more scientific and humane ways. Thoughts of "Abby" and her readers took up residence in my mind and, with time, I turned into a sort of Dear Abby myself, with one difference: I write in Arabic for Arab readers.

After I had been in California for two months our financial situation deteriorated and I found myself in the position of having to accept any job my limited English would allow in order to bring in a bit of money. With the help of a young Syrian I found work at a gas station. Once I had helped blood pump through the human heart; now I found myself pumping gas! Some may think I was embarrassed by my new job. On the contrary, I regarded it as a golden opportunity to acquire first-hand experience of all classes of American society instead of just reading about them in the "Dear Abby" column. I observed the actions and behavior of the gas station's clients, and listened to what they had to say. Some of them would start talking to me, and sometimes the conversation would branch out into personal matters.

On the whole I felt that people treated me with much more respect than when I was a doctor in Syria. Even when I made a mistake, I was treated well. One day, an American man who had lost his way came into the gas station and asked me if I knew the way to Knott Street. I indicated one of the shelves and told him he would find what he was looking for on it. He smiled politely at me, said, "thank you," and went on his way.

One of the other workers came over to me and asked if I had understood the customer's question. I replied that I thought he had asked for pistachio nuts. When I realized I had misunderstood the question I was embarrassed, but the customer's smile and words of thanks still warm my heart today. The fact that I received more respect as a foreign gas station attendant in America than as a doctor in my native land still stuns me and was the thing that took me and shook me by the shoulders. All of the questions I had regarding the morality of our culture and belief system became more pressing, and—as I pumped gas and talked to scores of Americans every day—my need for answers grew more and more urgent.

A year after my arrival, several days before Christmas, Texaco threw a holiday party for its gas station workers at the Hilton Hotel. When I arrived at the party and saw the gaily decorated hall and the carefully arranged tables of food, and saw how we workers—non-English-speaking foreigners, for the most part—were welcomed, I burst into tears. I ran to the ladies' room to hide my tears and my feelings, but when I came back I felt that the woman sitting beside me had sensed my confusion, as she asked what had upset me. I pointed at another woman and said, "That lady over there looks like my sister in Syria whom I haven't seen for a year," then dissolved into tears once more. But it was not the memory of my sister that made me cry, but the recollection—in the midst of a joyous celebration of the birth of another God—of a homeland that had a mandate from its God to prey upon its women and its poor.

I gave birth to another daughter, Angela, after I had been in the United States for a year and a half. She was only forty days old when I welcomed my two other children, whom I had left be-hind in Syria, at the Los Angeles airport. Our happiness was complete that day when our American dream came true and we seemed to be embarking upon a more settled and produc-tive life. The day my two eldest children started school paved my way into American society. My son, Mazen, who was nine at the time, went into the fourth grade, while our four-year-old daughter Farah started nursery school. By involving myself in their school lives I discovered a world totally different from the one in which I had been brought up. I, too, learned many valu-able lessons from the people who taught my children.

Mazen suffered from congenital hearing loss. When we lived in Syria, despite being a doctor, I could not afford to buy hearing aids for him, as these were not produced locally and had to be imported from Europe. At the time Syria had no trade relations with the West, as it had been the subject of an international boycott ever since it had been accused of support-ing terrorism. At the school's suggestion, Mazen was sent to see an ear specialist, and within less than a week he was using his hearing aids. I shall never forget the day we left the clinic with Mazen wearing the aids for the first time, beaming all over his face and twittering away like a little bird, "Mommy, can you believe it! I can hear the cars in the street." I threw myself sobbing into my husband's arms and he shouted, "Long live America! Long live America!"

We decided to celebrate that same day and went to a restau-rant that I still remember was called Tom's Hamburger, not far from our home in Paramount. We chose it because it was the cheapest place to go. A hamburger in those days cost 69 cents, and the hour we spent in that restaurant was the happiest of our lives. As we sat around the table we began to play a game in which Farah stood behind Mazen and whispered a word in his ear. If he heard her, he got a dime, and if he did not, Farah got one. I noticed that Farah tried to pronounce the words in such a way as to ensure that her brother would hear them, even though this meant forfeiting her 10 cents.

About a week later a woman called me, introduced herself as Nadja Ellis, and told me that Los Angeles Unified School District had appointed her to be Mazen's special teacher, and she would concentrate on helping Mazen with his speech, language comprehension, and vocabulary to ensure that these would improve over time. With time Ms. Ellis became a member of the family. She helped our entire family overcome our linguistic deficiencies and enabled us to keep in touch with the school. Ms. Scarf, Mazen's home-room teacher, was no less involved in Mazen's life than Ms. Ellis was and she took as great an interest in him. Mazen would come home from school bursting with excitement and tell me, "Mommy, can you believe it, Ms. Scarf hugs me every day. Why didn't the teachers in Syria ever hug me?" My child's questions etched themselves painfully and deeply on my mind and spirit, and I would reply silently: I'm still searching for answers myself, little one.

One day I went to pick Farah up from school at the end of the day and found her in the schoolyard with her teacher sitting next to her, helping her tie her shoelaces. As I stood watching them from some distance away, the sight of the two of them together revived old memories, bitter ones, still lodged deep in my mind. I remembered my head teacher when I was Farah's age. He came up to me at break time and asked me to leave school and deliver a package of bread he had bought to his home for him. Fearful, I stammered out naïvely: "But we've got dictation now." I had barely finished the sentence before he slapped me in the face as hard as he could. Remembering that sting of that cruel slap, I went up to Mrs. Anderson to thank her for her kindness and she said, "I saw her running toward the gate with her shoelaces undone and I was afraid she'd trip over them." Mrs. Anderson hugged Farah and said, patting her on the shoulder, "Be a good girl, now. I'll see you tomorrow." I watched Farah's face in the rearview mirror as she sat in the back seat. Her eyes were darting glances all around her, and I thought to myself: How I envy you, little one. Why did fate not give me a teacher like Mrs. Anderson when I was a girl—not to tie my shoelaces, but to bandage my wounds?

When I got home I finished writing an article I had begun a couple of days earlier, and concluded it with the words: "Our Prophet Muhammad says: 'Teach your children to pray at the age of seven and beat them if they don't at the age of ten.' To Hell with a prophet who demands that a father beat his ten-year-old son to make him pray to God!"

One day Mr. Wilson, the head teacher, telephoned me and said, "Mrs. Sultan, Mazen's left his hearing aids at home. Could you bring them to the school?" I thanked him for calling and told him, "Of course, I'll be there at once!" I was late, though, in getting the hearing aids to the school, but when I opened the door to go out to the car I saw the head teacher holding Mazen by the hand as they walked together toward our house. When he saw me, Mr. Wilson said, "Mrs. Sultan, I know you're busy, so I decided to walk with Mazen on this beautiful spring day so that we could pick up the hearing aids ourselves." Mr. Wilson did not want me to feel guilty for not having brought my son's hearing aids sooner, and insisted that he had decided to come along himself just to enjoy the beautiful weather.

I gave him the hearing aids and went back to my desk to note down on a few scraps of paper a story I remembered having read in a Muslim book about Caliph Omar Ibn al-Khattab. The caliph hit his son over the head with his stick for no particular reason, and, when his wife Hafsa protested and asked him, "Why did you hit him?," Omar replied, "I saw he was getting above himself and decided to cut him down to size." I followed this story with an account of what had happened to me that day and concluded the article with the words: "Long live America and down with the culture of injustice, oppression, and persecution! Long live Mr. Wilson, and everlasting death to Caliph Omar Ibn al-Khattab!"

As a result of the great kindness the teachers showed to my children, I became profoundly involved in my children's lives at school, not only in order to support them throughout their education, but also so that I could learn together with them. I used to sign up for every school field trip, adding my name to the list of parents who volunteered to help the teacher escort the students. I often volunteered to help the children across dangerous streets when the crossing guard was absent for one reason or another, and I have kept many of the certificates of appreciation for this that I received from my children's schools.

I remember how once, when my husband was at work, I discovered that we had run out of milk. At that time a gallon of milk cost $1.69, and, search as I did, I could come up with only $1.68. I asked Mazen to go to the shop across the street and tell the shopkeeper—a very nice woman who knew me well—that I would pay the missing penny next time. But Mazen refused, saying that he would be embarrassed. I was at a loss to know what to do. My small daughter Angela was asleep and I could not leave the house. Then suddenly I had a brainstorm, and told Mazen, "Listen, go to the shop, but before you go inside look around the parking lot and see if you can find a penny that someone's dropped. If you find one, add it to the money you've got, and that's the problem solved. If you can't find one, come back home." Mazen danced for joy at the idea, took the $1.68, and ran over to the shop.

Just a few minutes later I saw him through the window coming back carrying a gallon of milk and laughing out loud. When I opened the door for him I was surprised to hear him say, "Mommy, you'll never believe what happened! I was look-ing for a cent and I found a dollar bill, so now I've got ninety-nine cents," and he tossed me the change he had in his hand. I caught him by the shoulder and said, "Listen, honey, that's America for you: You ask it for a cent and it gives you a dollar—but you have to go out and look for it!"

In Mazen's first year at California State Polytechnic Univer-sity, Pomona, he submitted a request for financial aid from the federal government to cover his university expenses. I had al-ready promised him that, once he had obtained the grant, his father and I would do everything in our power to pay for every-thing else. We did not expect this financial aid to cover all his tuition fees, and on the day he was due to pay them he went off to university with an open check signed by me to pay for the rest. A few hours later he telephoned me and told me, laugh-ing, "Mommy, guess what happened!" "What?" I asked. "That's

America," he said, "You ask it for a cent and it gives you a dollar. The grant covered all the tuition fees and the cost of the books and I've still got some money left." When he got home he tossed me the check I had given him, saying jokingly, "I don't want your help, America's more generous that you are!" I caught him by the shoulder and told him, "Listen, this is a debt that will have to be repaid when you graduate," but before I could finish my sentence he completed it for me: "And I have to donate a hearing aid to Los Angeles Unified School District whenever I can so that it can be given to a needy child—I know that. I know all that. I've got the lesson down by heart!"

Of course, there was always a contradiction in our lives that worried me: We were foreigners from the Middle East living in the United States. At the time of the first Gulf War Mazen had been in the U.S. for little more than a year. I observed him as he watched events unfold on the television and tried to give his sister Farah his own childish explanation of what was happening: "We Americans are stronger than Saddam Hussein and we'll crush the Iraqis." I tried to hide my tears. There was a discrepancy there between the first half of his remark, "we Americans" and the second, "we'll crush the Iraqis," and it stopped me in my tracks. But, undaunted, I moved forward.

Once I realized that my English—and my reading comprehension in particular—had improved sufficiently to allow me to do so, I decided to take the medical equivalency examinations I had to pass in order to validate my qualifications and enable me to practice medicine in the United States. Among the subjects I had to obtain a pass in were behavioral science and psychiatry. Both these subjects plunged me into an ocean of knowledge the like of which I had never previously encountered, and made me feel embarrassed at the superficiality of my level of medical expertise in this field—not as a result of any personal inadequacy, but because of the limited information available on the subject to those who studied at our universities. I believe limitations were imposed because much of this material conflicted with many of the teachings of Islam, and it was kept from students for fear that contact with it would change their way of thinking. Through Kaplan Medical, a school that helped foreign doctors to pass these exams, I met other doctors from Muslim countries such as Iran and Pakistan, and they confirmed that they had not studied these subjects at such a high level or in such great depth at their universities either.

My thirst for knowledge of these two subjects spurred me to delve into them more deeply than was strictly necessary to pass the exams in them. Very early in my life in America I became fascinated by books that dealt with behavioral science and mental health, and I set out to quench my thirst for this knowledge. One day I made to my husband a remark he still remembers: "Now I know why America is a superpower. America is great because its people enjoy freedom of thought. They are the product of a culture that was born in the laboratory under the scientist's lens, while we in the Muslim world lag behind because we have come from a repressive culture that has no respect for the mind and refuses to acknowledge its [own] failure to come to grips with science."

My reading, though, ranged far beyond the books and articles I needed to read in order to pass the medical equivalency exams. When I discovered the existence of an Arabic-language press printed and published in California, I was delighted. In great hope and expectation I set out at once to look for these newspapers and read them. I expected that the freedom we enjoyed in America would allow us to express things we had previously repressed, and air opinions we had kept bottled up— only to discover little by little that these newspapers were a carbon copy of our press in the Arab world. Each paper is supported by a specific country or party, and the struggle between the newspapers closely resembles the struggles we experienced in our homelands.

At that point slender threads still bound me to Islam. I decided to embark upon a free search for the lost truth, in hopes of perhaps replacing these threads with a sturdy rope. I began my research on two different planes—the Muslim plane, which enabled me to gain a more profound and intimate knowledge of Islam without the fears induced by social pressures, and the American plane, so as to acquire a deeper firsthand knowledge of American society, too, which would allow me to compare what I had learned about both.

While engaged in this research I did not stop writing for so much as a day, and began to compose an article more or less every week. In these brief essays I calmly expressed very mild criticism of our customs and education methods, supporting my position with comparisons with what I had read and observed in the United States. Every article was like a stone thrown into still waters: Each one made waves and as, over time, I became increasingly critical and outspoken, they generated an increasing number of reactions. If the development of my writing in the period between early 1989, when my first article was published, and September 10, 2001, were to be plotted on a graph, a slow but steady rise would be observed in the line that represents the severity of my criticism. Each point along that line would reflect the extent to which my way of thinking and my attitude to Islam had changed, and record precisely when that change took place.

I became addicted to reading both Islamic and American books, and the more assiduously I read, the more I discovered that our tragic condition in the Muslim world, as compared with that of the United States, is simply the sad result of our Islamic belief system. I had expected that the slender thread, which during the first four years of my life in America had continued to bind me to Islam, would be replaced with a sturdy rope, only to discover day by day that it had become more fragile than ever. I moved from one newspaper to another, as each one banished me, sending me to the next. The Saudi-supported paper was the first to turn down my work. I was then adopted by a paper supported at the time by Saddam Hussein's government—not because they liked what I wrote, but because they hated the Saudis.

After his defeat in the first Gulf War, Saddam Hussein tried to use Islam as a lever to win the trust of his people and save his regime from collapse, and so I did not last long at that newspaper either, and ended up writing for a paper supported by the Syrian Embassy in Washington. As the Syrian government, like Saddam Hussein's, initially, can hardly be accused of being religiously inclined, my presence in the pages of this newspaper was a little more prolonged. A problem did crop up later, however, because the publisher was a Christian, and after a certain point he, as a non-Muslim, could no longer withstand the increasingly vehement attacks launched against my articles in his paper by the Muslim diaspora.

Muslims withdrew their advertisements from the paper in protest against what I wrote, and the publisher called me about two months before the September 11th terrorist attack to ask me if he could give my telephone number to CAIR (the Council on American-Islamic Relations) because one of its members wanted to talk to me. I agreed, of course, and that same day I received a telephone call from Mr. Hussam Ayloush of CAIR. Mr. Ayloush was courteous and did his best to restrain himself during our conversation. He expressed his displeasure at what I had written and said that I had come close to overstepping the line. When a Muslim—especially if he is a member of CAIR—tells a writer that he or she has come close to overstepping the line, his words, naturally, carry a veiled threat whose dangers can be understood only by those with an excellent command of Arabic and a profound understanding of Islam. After they heard what he had said, a number of my loyal friends asked me to ease up and be patient, as things did not bode well. I began to boil internally like a pressure cooker, and, as my temperature rose, I felt I was about to explode.

I often look back and wonder, where did my resolve come from? There were so many incidents, but one memory comes back to me from the time I left Syria. My husband left for America about a year before I did. When I submitted a request for a passport for my children, the officer at the emigration and permits department refused to give me one on the grounds that, under Islamic law, I was not my children's legal guardian and that it was up to their father to submit the request. I took from my bag the power of attorney which my husband had obtained from the appropriate authorities and which legally authorized me to dispose of his money, his possessions, and all his affairs, but the officer handed it back to me, saying, "That's a power of attorney, not proof of guardianship. It gives you the right to dispose of his property, but you do not have guardianship of his children."

"But they are my children, too, sir."

"A woman is not the guardian of her children. Do you understand?"

"What can we do now? Please, I need their passports and their father isn't here."

"The only solution is for you to bring a man from your husband's family who will declare that he permits you the right to obtain a passport for your children." Only one member of my husband's immediate family lived in the same town as we did, and I had never met him in my life. Ali was an alcoholic notorious for his ill nature and poor character, because of which my husband had never wanted to introduce him to me.

I inquired about him and was directed to his home in a poor quarter far from where we lived. His wife greeted us with a warm smile, and signs of compassion for me could be read in her face. Very quietly, for fear of being overheard, she whispered in my ear: "He's drunk all the time. I don't know if he'll agree to do what you ask. Try to bribe him with a bit of money. He won't take in what you say, but the sight of the money may bring him round."

At the emigration and permits department, after I'd stuffed fifty Syrian pounds (one dollar) into his pocket, Ali approached the officer in charge, holding out his identity card, which proved he belonged to my husband's family—without specifying the closeness of the relationship—and said, "Yes officer. She's my brother's wife, and my brother has appointed me guardian of his children. In accordance with my brother's wishes I shall not prevent her from acquiring passports for his children." When we left the building I had the passports in my hand, but the anger grew inside me. A knowledgeable and respectable woman and a doctor, I was not considered fit to be the guardian of my own children, but a drunkard of no moral worth had the right, for one dollar, to become my guardian and the guardian of my children.

I fled my prison with suitcases containing nothing more than painful memories. I was leaving my two children behind and would send for them when their father and I were able to support them. Packed in my suitcases with the love I held for my children were the faces of Suha, Fatima, Amal, and thousands of other women whose tragedies, had I decided to write about them, would fill too many books to fit into the American Library of Congress. I left for America spurred on by a single aim: To defend those Allah had cut down in size until they were smaller than flies. I had the aim and the will, but I lacked any clear vision or plan which would enable me to attain my goal. But, America re-formed me, armed me with knowledge, clarified my vision, and helped me to outline my plan to save those victims. I decided to bring "Allah" to justice on criminal charges.

8.

"Who is that woman on Al Jazeera?"

THAT'S WHAT EVERYONE in the Arab world starting asking: "Who is that woman on Al Jazeera who told a man to be quiet so that *she* could speak?" At the time, I had no idea the firestorm I had ignited. When I think back to my first appearance on Al Jazeera, I am still stunned and can't believe what I did. In my first appearance with the Al Jazeera television network, I debated a Muslim clergyman named X who was not all that different from the preacher in our local mosque. The program's host called me two days ahead of time to ask if I could take part. He didn't explain what the program was like, but said, "We'd like to hear your opinion on the extent of the connection between Islamic teachings and terrorism." I had not carried on a conversation in literary Arabic for almost sixteen years. During that time I had written that form of Arabic but had not spoken it. I had no idea what the program was like, as I don't have Al Jazeera on my cable list and I'm not a fan of television in general.

Of course, Al Jazeera had good reason for choosing me. My essays were well known all over the Arab world. My opinions on the subject were clear and precise. They chose me so that they could show Arab viewers how superficial my attitude was, discredit me, and confirm that I was incapable of defending my opinions. They were convinced that even though, as a writer, I was able to assert my views to my readers, I would prove virtually incapable of doing so on television, where I would be knocked out with one decisive blow. The number of television viewers in the Arab world is much larger than the number of readers, and it includes all classes of Muslim Arab society. If I were to be shown up as a failure before this audience, they thought it would really be the end of me!

The general public in the Arab world tends, in the main, to judge any discussion by the same criteria my mother used to evaluate the preacher in our local mosque: by vocal stridency and volume. The other guest on the program was a talented preacher skilled in the arts of bellowing and raiding. He did not allow me one quarter of the time allocated to me. He did not respect my right to reply, nor did he respect my time as the philosophy of raiding believes neither in rights nor in privacy. His shouting and raging robbed me of the time allocated to me. He did not hear a word I said, nor did he reply to a single question I asked.

Calmly and with what I thought was exceptional patience I managed to express my thoughts, and within a short time I had stated my opinion to the viewers clearly and succinctly. Never in the history of Islam has a woman vied with a man's ability to raid and shout. Never in the history of Islam has a woman silenced a man's clamor with her calmness or overcome his shouts by her ability to talk and convince. The philosophy of raiding at which Muslim men so excel failed for the first time in its history, defeated by a woman who had not held a conversation in literary Arabic for sixteen years and who was speaking to an audience of millions of Muslims for the first time.

As our time began to run out, the program's host gave me another few seconds to conclude what I had to say and summarize my opinions, but the raiding guest interrupted me once more. Time seemed too short and too precious for me to waste even a second of it, and I shouted at him: "Be quiet! It's my turn!" I uttered this sentence without realizing that it would open a new chapter in Arab and Muslim history. Never in the history of Islam has a woman clearly and forcefully asked a Muslim man to be quiet because it was her turn to speak. Women in Islamic custom and tradition don't have a turn. They have no time that is theirs alone. Women in Islam don't even possess their own selves, or the right to make their own decisions.

My mailbox was flooded with letters. The statement "Be quiet, it's my turn" was the subject of most of these. Viewers who supported my position praised what I had said and considered it to have been one of the best things I had said during the debate. But Muslim men who saw it as a threat to their ability to raid and shout cursed me and regarded my courage to say it as a disgraceful impertinence. What is important to me is that I broke a taboo that other Muslim women may have seen me break. I broke a taboo I do not observe and which I do not regard as sacrosanct, and I hope that it encourages other women to follow in my footsteps. I challenged the insolence of a Muslim sheikh and exposed his shallowness and hypocrisy for the first time in fourteen centuries.

Who was I to perform such a feat? What I did made me begin to wonder just who I was and what I believed in. Who was that woman on Al Jazeera? I am a Muslim woman. Yes, I think of myself as a Muslim, whether or not I believe in Islam. I did not choose to be a Muslim, but it is not within my power to make myself anything else. Each one of us is whoever she is persuaded to be in her early years. Each one of us has fallen into the trap set for him in childhood, and the rest of his life is no more than a bitter struggle either to stay in that trap or leave it. The decision to stay or go is yours alone and life challenges every one of us no matter what we do. If you decide to stay, life will present you with challenges which will drag you out of it, and if you decide to leave it will challenge you to remain. Staying is a challenge, and leaving is a challenge. One's freedom lies in your decision to stay or go.

I fell into the trap of Islam in the early years of my childhood. When I grew older, I decided to escape from that trap. My freedom lies in my decision. I don't believe that I will ever be able to free myself completely from the jaws of that trap—no one can—but my inability to do so does not detract from my freedom. I am free now, whether I manage to free myself completely or only partially.

That's life's game. Every person is born with a sort of birthmark, which others have prepared for him. He plays no part in deciding what that birthmark looks like or the elements it's made up of, but he finds himself forced to wear it, imprinted on his flesh, throughout his lifetime, as it can never be completely removed and it can never completely fade. Each birthmark contains a person's family's values, principles, customs, and traditions. This is all you possess, and all you have with which to confront life's challenges. Some parts of it will impede you; others will make your path smoother. You alone will decide what to keep and what to get rid of. Life isn't fair. Why?

Each person's birthmark differs from the next. What Margaret Thatcher found in her birthmark in no way resembled what my grandmother found in hers. Mrs. Thatcher found things that smoothed her way to becoming prime minister of Great Britain. Its motto said, "You can be anything you want to be." In the course of her life, Mrs. Thatcher faced a great many challenges that placed obstacles in her path, but by staying true to the mark she received at birth, she managed to overcome these challenges.

My grandmother's birthmark was different. What my grandmother found enabled her to dance for joy at her husband's wedding to a second wife while dying of sadness inside. The motto inscribed on her birthmark was different. It said, "Women are defective. Marriage will conceal one tenth of that defect, and the grave will hide the other nine tenths." My grandmother could have refused to dance at her husband's wedding, but she chose to obey his orders and continue as his wife under his protection, so that marriage would conceal some of her defect. The game life played with Margaret Thatcher was less rough than the game it played with my grandmother. Mrs. Thatcher was convinced that she was fit to be prime minister, while my grandmother was convinced that she was fit only to be my grandfather's wife.

Life presented both women with challenges designed to make them renounce their convictions, but my grandmother faced challenges that made it much more difficult for her to give up her beliefs than it was for Margaret Thatcher. Let's assume for the sake of argument that Mrs. Thatcher, discouraged by the challenges she faced, decided to renounce her conviction that she could be whoever she wanted to be. Renouncing this conviction would have deprived her of the office to which she aspired, but she would not have ended up homeless on the streets. In Margaret Thatcher's unconscious that conviction would have gone on nagging at her until she used it to become, if not exactly what she had wanted, at least something close to what she had wanted.

And let's assume for the sake of argument that my grandmother, for her part, had decided to renounce her conviction that women are a defect of which marriage covers up one tenth. Her renunciation of that conviction would have helped her refuse my grandfather's orders and avoid the pain that dancing at his wedding caused her. But had she done that she would have ended up in her father's house, a disgrace to herself and her family.

In my grandmother's unconscious this conviction would have continued to nag at her, just as Mrs. Thatcher's did. Never in all her life, even when things were at their best, did my grandmother ever become anything more than a small portion of that defect which she had been persuaded she embodied.

The birthmarks we inherit remains etched into the depths of our unconscious, and however we may try to remove it, a large scar will remain to affect us and remind us. And so I repeat: I am a Muslim. In the realm of my conscious mind I exercised my freedom and decided to leave Islam, but to what extent have I succeeded in freeing my unconscious from the birthmark which has been imprinted upon it? There is still a huge scar barring my way.

I ask myself again, "Who is that woman on Al Jazeera?,"

and I can only answer, as my grandmother might have because of the lessons of Islam: "She is defective! She is grateful to her husband for covering up one tenth of this defect of hers and is waiting for the grave to hide the other nine tenths." We know from modern studies in neurobiology that the birthmark, as I'm calling it, is accompanied by anatomical, chemical, and physiological changes in the cells and tissues of the brain. I don't know if I have the capacity to re-program myself, but I know one thing: I don't want my daughters' birthmarks to affect them in the same way I am affected by the one my mother gave me.

I hope what I write here can help other Muslims think about the marks they pass on to their children before those children are born. I suffered because of the contents of my inherited birthmark; I am still suffering and will continue to do so until my dying day. But, to a certain extent, I have managed to spare my daughters some of that suffering. My daughters may not be able to become a Margaret Thatcher, but I have not the slightest doubt that they will be more like Mrs. Thatcher than like my grandmother. Nor do I have the slightest doubt that my granddaughter will be able to be a Margaret Thatcher if she wants. I rejected my inherited birthmark, not solely out of compassion for myself, but out of compassion for future generations.

Again, I ask myself, "Who is that woman on Al Jazeera?" She says that she is a Muslim woman. But what is a Muslim woman? She is whoever Islam tells her she is in her early years. What motto does Islam painfully inscribe on her birthmark? "A woman is a defect." This hadith pronounced by Islam's prophet, Muhammad, was handed down mother to daughter, inscribed on one birthmark and then the next and then the next until it reached me. Millions of other traditions have accumulated around this one simple hadith, and these have not only hallowed it but have made it uglier.

In Islam, this hadith and all its ramifications are sacred: We are forbidden to overstep it, cast doubts on it, or question it. There is no more deadly conviction on earth to a woman than the conviction that she is a defect, and no other belief can make it any less offensive. I heard this belief repeated from my first moment of awareness. This was not the only hadith that dropped into my package, but it was the ugliest.

My earliest memory of my mother is her story of how she chose my name. She laughed when she told me the story, but I always wondered if she was crying inside. She told me she was not very happy at my arrival, and neither was my father, needless to say. My paternal uncle's wife had already had two boys before she did. Under pressure from this calamity my mother was at a loss as to what name to give me. One morning my paternal uncle was passing by the veranda of our house when he saw my mother carrying me in her arms. He greeted her and asked: "Haven't you chosen a name for her yet?"

My mother replied: "Not yet. Do you have any suggestions?"

My uncle said without hesitation: "Call her 'Shit,' it's the only name she deserves."

My mother told this story hundreds of times when I was within earshot. She would tell it jokingly to amuse her female friends from the neighborhood, unaware of how deeply she hurt me each time she said it. And so, to my birthmark, my mother added the name Shit at the behest of my uncle. Her own birthmark, however, handed down through the centuries dictated her treatment of me.

The most terrifying thing about a Muslim woman's birthmark is that part which comes from the Prophet's stories about his wives that create a trap every Muslim woman falls into: No man in my life can be better than his Prophet and I cannot be less obedient to him than his Prophet's wives were to their husband. Men have internalized their Prophet, and women have internalized his wives.

How can the men and women of Islam escape from this trap? I'm not sure they can unless they are willing to look critically at some of these marriages, not as an affront to Muhammad or his wives, but to help explain a Muslim man's attitude toward women and his treatment of them, given that Muhammad is their ideal.

The Koran says: "There is a good example in Allah's apostle" (33:21). The Prophet contracted his marriage with Aisha when she was six years old and he was fifty. The marriage was consummated when she was nine. Bint al-Shati's *Wives of Muhammad*, a biography of the Prophet describes that day for us in Aisha's words:

"The Prophet married me when I was six years old and the marriage was consummated when I was nine. The Prophet of God came to our home in company with men and women who were among his followers. My mother came [to me] while I was in a swing between the branches of a tree and made me come down. She smoothed my hair, wiped my face with a little water then came forward and led me to the door. She stopped me while I calmed myself a little. Then she took me in. The Prophet of God was sitting on a bed in our home, and she sat me in his lap. Everyone jumped up and went out, and the Prophet consummated his marriage with me at our home."

It is not because of its historical value that this story deserves space in my book. Rather, I want to discuss its moral importance and what it has done, and is still doing, to destroy the moral and mental fiber of Muslim men and women. A fifty-year-old man marries a six-year-old girl and consummates their marriage when she turns nine. This is a crime, pure and simple. It may not have been one at the time it happened, but the time has come for it to be considered as such. The ugliness of this crime does not lie only in the event itself, but in the religious and legal legitimization it has been accorded. It is the moral examples the individual Muslim extracts from this incident which invest it with its importance and gravity, not its time or place.

Islamic custom attaches no value to childhood. A child is his father's property, who has the right to dispose of him as he would of any other property. When a mother picks up her young daughter of no more than nine years and places her in the arms of a man her grandfather's age, her daughter's childhood has been irreparably violated. When the mother's action acquired religious and legal legitimacy, it became a way of life for fourteen centuries.

A child in the Muslim world has no rights. He is a piece of property, not a responsibility. Islamic teachings persuade Muslim children that their parents must be obeyed because they gave them life, but the same teachings tell the parents nothing of their responsibility for the quality and nature of that child's life. Muslim education focuses on convincing the child of the necessity of blind obedience to his parents. He obeys their every command, save those that prevent him from obeying God. Allah gets hold of people through their parents and then goes even further: To guarantee the ogre's control of the child, it orders him to disobey his parents when their orders do not accord with its own.

Islamic law touches on society's responsibility toward children in only one instance: If a child's parents leave Islam, society must intervene and restore the child to the Muslim fold. People in Muslim society fall, from earliest childhood, into their parents' trap and live at their mercy, in the absence of any law that gives society the right to intervene to protect them from their parents' tyranny. This situation continues throughout their lives. A Muslim man remains a child in his father's eyes for as long as that father lives, and the only opportunity he gets to exercise his male authority is by keeping a firm hold over his wife and children.

The cycle of torment continues until you don't know where it begins or ends. When a Muslim woman marries, she marries not just a man, but his father and mother, too, who, under Muslim law, play a major role in their marriage. The parents intervene in every matter, large or small, and the mother-in-law uses this situation as an opportunity to play the role denied to her earlier in life, frequently pouring her anger out on her daughter-in-law in order to exact her revenge for when she herself was a daughter-in-law. The young husband regards himself as legally and traditionally obliged to obey his mother blindly, and allows her to do as she likes as she interferes, arbitrarily and without restraint, in his life and that of his family.

A Muslim man unconsciously assumes the role his own father played and rules his wife with an iron hand while simultaneously feeling guilty for the oppression his mother suffered at his father's hands when she was young. He justifies the situation by telling himself that he is giving her the right to take revenge for what she has suffered. His mother, in her unconscious mind, is imitating the role of her own mother-in-law as she vents the pain of her own youth on her daughter-in-law—and so the cycle continues as Islam uses women as a tool to oppress other women. Women in a society of this kind cannot themselves take revenge on men for having oppressed them, but they can vent their pent-up anger on other women.

I get a lot of letters from Muslim women who curse me. I cannot explain this reaction of one woman to another by anything other than an expression of jealousy which devours them. When they read my essays, these women ask themselves, both consciously and unconsciously: "Why can Wafa Sultan exercise her freedom to express her opinions while I cannot? Why can Wafa Sultan live in a country that respects her as a woman while I cannot?" When they become frustrated by lack of an answer to their questions, they attack and curse me. I understand and respect their position. Perhaps even better than that, I empathize with them. My heart breaks because I know what a terrible life they lead, but the only thing I can do about it is to write and speak out. Perhaps, in the way I speak out against Islam, I can help them get out of the trap they find themselves in.

The story of Muhammad's marriage to Aisha helps perpetuate this oppression to this very day. My sister decided to marry her daughter to the son of her paternal aunt when she was eleven years old and he was forty. I was an adolescent at the time and I can still remember my sister's response to the women of the neighborhood when they asked her what her daughter thought of this marriage. "She's still young, she'll come to love him as time goes by. It's a marriage in accordance with the law of God and his Prophet." Alas, that never came to be. The marriage was a horrible and unhappy one that she was never able to escape. When my niece ran away from her husband, as she often did, and went back to her father's home, she discovered that she had merely fled from one corner of her prison to another. Her father persuaded her that the best place for a woman is her husband's house and, under pressure from her family, she went back to "the best place designated for her by God and his Prophet." My niece, seeing no other way out, committed suicide at the age of twenty-six, by which time she was the mother of four children.

The story of Muhammad's marriage to Aisha has a further and more horrifying effect on the relationship between Muslim men and women. In the story of the marriage, Muhammad pounced upon the nine-year-old Aisha the moment her mother placed her in his arms on a bed in her own home. Through the story of this "marriage," Islam denies women the right to reach the stage of physical, intellectual, and emotional maturity at which they are fully ready to marry. It denies Muslim women the right to marry as a rational human being. That a girl should jump from her swing and become within a few minutes a mature woman in the arms of a man—this is something the most basic laws of morality cannot accept. The great misfortune is that this incident has been sanctioned by both religious and secular law and has become a way of life.

Under this law the childhood of many young girls is violated throughout the Islamic world. In many Arab countries such as Jordan, Syria, and Egypt, hundreds of crimes are committed every year against the rights of underage girls, who have no control over their lives, by men from the Arabian Gulf states. These men with their illicit money and their nonexistent morals take advantage of the poverty running rampant in these countries to buy minors for money. For each girl purchased by one of these monstrous pigs, it is the beginning of a journey of suffering, which usually ends with the underage girl being returned to her family after her childhood, her womanhood, her honor, and her reputation violated in exchange for trifling sums of money, in the name of marriage in accordance with the law of God and his Prophet. The minor returns to the hell of her life after she's been abandoned in a society, which does not respect her plight. If she is able, she lives out the rest of her days as a morsel to be chewed over, mercilessly and without embarrassment, in the mouths of others.

There are other marriages of Muhammad's, such as his marriage to Zeinab, that are ruinous to the proper relationship between a man and a woman. Zeinab was the daughter of Muhammad's paternal aunt and the wife of his adopted son Zeid, hence his daughter-in-law. One day the Prophet went to Zeid and Zeinab's home. The doorway was covered by a cowhide curtain which the wind lifted, allowing him to see Zeinab unveiled in her room. He was moved with admiration for her. Zeinab invited Muhammad to come in, but he refused and retraced his steps, murmuring: "Praised be He who changes hearts." When Zeid learned from his wife what had happened, he went to Muhammad and told him: "Perhaps Zeinab pleased you and I should leave her to you." Muhammad told him: "Keep your wife." When you think about it, what we have just witnessed is a son who is passing his wife along to his father as if he was asking a friend of his, "Do you like my shoes? Shall I take them off so that you can have them?" Since this "sanctified" marriage took place, women in Islam have been put on and taken off like shoes for centuries.

But, Muhammad was unable to resist his desires and the rock began to tumble down from the mountain peak, verse after verse, enabling him to give free rein to those desires, while the Angel Gabriel began to shuttle back and forth, up and down, until he had resolved Muhammad's dilemma. In the first of these verses from the Koran, God reprimanded Muhammad for having concealed his feelings: "You sought to hide in your heart what Allah was to reveal: you were afraid of man, although it would have been more right to fear Allah" (33:37). On his first journey Gabriel legislated for Muhammad to fall in love with a married woman, even though that woman was his daughter-in-law. Then the second verse rolled down, which ordered him to marry Zeinab: "And when Zeid satisfied his desire, we gave her to you in marriage" (33:37). Marriage to the wife of an adopted son was not acceptable in pre-Islamic Arab society, and a third verse conveniently descended in order to invalidate Zeid's adoption and deter those who were beginning to criticize

Muhammad's marriage to his daughter-in-law. "Muhammad is the father of no man among you. He is the apostle of Allah and the Seal of the Prophets" (33:40).

The Muslim male, as portrayed here, is a poor soul who cannot control his instincts and, therefore, has the right to give them free rein in any manner he chooses. When God's Prophet coveted his adopted son's wife and God ordered him to satisfy that desire, this behavior, for Muslims, became enshrined in both religious and secular law. Muhammad banned adoption in order to justify his socially unacceptable marriage—by the standards of the time—to the wife of his adopted son. This ban put an end to a social system that at the time helped save many children who, for one reason or another, had been left fatherless, and the ban, to this day, continues to rot the soul of Muslim societies.

Many children who have lost their mothers or fathers in these societies end up as victims for whom no just solution can be found. The father's new wife in these societies neither regards nor treats her husband's children from another wife as if they were her own. Her belief in her faith, which bans adoption, prevents her, both consciously and unconsciously, from treating them warmly; new husbands behave similarly toward the children of their wife's first marriage. Orphanages in these societies are nothing more than corrals where even life's most basic moral principles are not observed. Society regards these children with contempt, as most of them are the offspring of extramarital relations. Revenge is taken on their fathers through them, and people refuse to adopt them because of their belief in Islamic law, which forbids adoption yet proposes no alternative. We all remember the disaster that faced the world in the wake of the war in Bosnia. Some 30,000 children were born illegitimately in the course of this war and, as their Muslim mothers refused to take care of them, they were distributed to Western countries, with the United States taking the lion's share. No Muslim country offered to take in a single one of these children.

Of all Muhammad's marriages, however, his marriage to Safia was the most horrific of all. Safia Bint Hayi was a Jewish woman whose husband, father, and brother Muhammad had killed when raiding the Khaybar tribe. She was taken prisoner in the course of the raid by one of Muhammad's men named Sahm. Muhammad took Safia from him, gave him seven other female prisoners as compensation, and married Safia the same day he killed her husband, brother, and father. Once again, a woman is given no opportunity to make a decision regarding her marriage or, ultimately, her fate. Safia finds herself in Muhammad's arms from one day to the next and does not have the right to accept or refuse what he decides to do with her.

When discussing the deteriorating position of women in the Muslim world some defenders of Muslim law protest, claiming that Islam revered women, but that some of its followers had misunderstood the Koran and the Prophetic tradition. But I still have a question: Have the same followers misunderstood the Prophet's attitude to women in his lifetime? Where are the Koranic verses or Prophetic traditions that can alleviate the ugliness of these attitudes? They are not to be found. How can we view the marriage of a fifty-year-old man to a six-year-old girl (consummated three years later) other than as rape? The answer is not to be found. How can we view the marriage of a man to his son's wife as an acceptable act? There is no passage to make one think otherwise. How can we view a man's marriage to his female captive after he has attacked her tribe and killed her husband, father, and brother except as a crime? We can't because there are no verses or traditions to persuade us otherwise.

In order to understand Islam's attitude to women, one has to think more deeply about the desert environment that gave birth to it. The tribe would go to sleep and wake to the rattle of the swords of another larger, better-equipped tribe. The raiding tribe would take the other tribe by storm, greedy for its land, its wealth, and its possessions. They would kill some of its men, and the rest would flee. Once the fires of battle had died down, the men of the victorious tribe would divide up the women from the defeated tribe among themselves just as they shared their livestock, possessions, and wealth. No tribe in Arab history was safe from raiding and its effects.

In addition to his fear of dying from hunger or thirst, a man in the Arabian Desert faced fear of another kind, a fear of which women were the source. He feared the disgrace he would suffer should she fall victim to another man. A woman, as far as a man of that time and place was concerned, was a constant reminder of his own failure and shame because he might fail in his attempts to defend her when his tribe was raided. Disgrace would fall on him, if she fell into the embrace of another man. His attitude toward her stemmed from his own feelings of inadequacy because of his possible inability to protect her. His hatred was not directed against the real wrongdoer responsible for his disgrace because he himself might one day be in the position of the raider, defeating another man and taking his women. Rather, his hatred was directed at a woman who might be his mother, his sister, or his wife. Since then there has been only one criterion by which Muslim male honor is measured: how well he protects the area between a woman's knees and her navel. He holds her responsible for this burden; subjected to shame, he is dishonored, and his treatment of her takes on the cast of a twisted sort of revenge.

Islam was born into an environment that sanctioned the capture and rape of women, holding them—not the man committing the crime—responsible. Islam did not proscribe what was already permissible. On the contrary, it legalized it and enshrined it in canonical law. Man's need to take his revenge on women because he considered them a source of disgrace was a pressing one, and his ogre legislated for him to satisfy that need. A large number of verses concerning women were revealed to its Prophet. These enormous boulders came down from the mountain to smash the heads of women, distorting their human form. Anyone who reads the Arabic literature, which describes the Prophet Muhammad's raids and how he distributed the booty and captives, will understand the nature of the trap into which Muslim men and their wives fell. Muhammad provides the example that Muslim men are supposed to imitate while Muslim women are supposed to take their example from his wives.

For fourteen centuries Muslim men have been unable to free themselves from the domination of their Prophet, and Muslim women have not managed to do better than his wives. Muhammad legalized for himself and his men the rape of the women captured in the course of their raids in a verse that tumbled down from the top of the mountain and fell into Muhammad's lap. The Koranic verse says: "Marry women who seem good to you: two, three or four of them. But if you fear you cannot maintain equality among them, marry one only" (4:3). Women who seem good to you? Men viewed marriage as nothing more than a response to their desires, without reference to the woman's feelings regarding the marriage. And men did not curb these desires, satisfying them with any woman he was able to acquire, just like so much chattel.

A man's wealth alone limited the number of women he was able to marry. The Koran distinguishes between two classes of woman: the free woman and the slave. The slave woman has no rights to freedom. Islam limits the number of free women a man may marry to four, if he can treat them all equally, and, if he cannot—to one. A slave woman does not enjoy the same rights as a free woman, and so a man may marry them as he pleases, so long as he can afford to buy them. What does Islam mean by equally? Equality in this case, in the Islamic sense of the word, means that the man must divide his sperm and his wealth equally among his four wives. If he cannot do this, he must take only one wife. How equitable the ogre is in what he accords to men and their oh-so-fortunate wives!

What have Muslim men and women got out of this complex "equitable" worldview that allows men to give free rein to their desires and turns women into a commodity to be bought in accordance with the requirements of those desires? Where is the concept of "family" or "children" in this dictionary that is so hard to read? Does either word have a definition in the Islamic lexicon? And what are the responsibilities of a man whose desires produce a whole army of children, as is the case with the family of Osama bin Laden, a man with innumerable brothers and sisters and a father who has had more wives than anyone can count?

Even if a Muslim man is able to give each of his four wives—and any other women he may have acquired—the same proportion of his property and his sperm, how can he divide his time and energies among the children who come into this world as the result of his unbridled desires? What price have we, as Muslim men and women, paid for this boulder that tumbled down from the top of that mountain? It has shattered us and torn a whole nation limb from limb, leaving the true concepts of "marriage" and "family" in ruins.

A Muslim man can see himself only in terms of his ability to pump out money and sperm. The Muslim woman, for her part, sees herself only as an incubator for his sperm and as a piece of furniture he has bought and paid for with his money. The man alone decides when to take possession of this object and when to deposit his sperm in it dictating a relationship in which human feelings have no value.

Because of a relationship that devalues true human feeling, the Muslim family is experiencing a crisis of love with children as its first victims. When my father courted my mother he was already a married man with five children, four girls and a boy. His excuse was that his wife was suffering from incurable tuberculosis. My grandfather agreed to the marriage without considering the feelings of my mother, who was only sixteen years old at the time. My father was forty. He argued that my father was a prosperous man of good reputation from a well-known family, and so he paid no attention to the opinion of my mother and grandmother. Women, he believed, should not be asked for their opinions in the same way one would not ask one's furniture for the answer to a question.

My father's first wife is said to have died neglected and forgotten in a hospital far out of town where tuberculosis sufferers were kept in isolation. My mother moved in to live with my father and his five children. His eldest daughter was one year older than my mother. In this vortex my mother lost her equilibrium and no longer knew if she were a wife, a mother of five, or one of his children, who looked on her as if she were one of their peers.

In the course of ten years she bore eight children. Although my father was by nature a peaceable and calm man who treated my mother well, I never saw my mother happy for so much as a day. She was not good at controlling life inside the home and the quarrels between her and her four stepdaughters continued day and night.

In that clamorous and teeming household I was born and lived the early years of my childhood. The nature of the relationship between my four half-sisters and my mother was a source of torment to me, as I was torn between the two opposing sides. My sisters got married to escape the way my mother treated them. A year after my youngest half-sister got married, just as our life seemed to be getting calmer, my father died suddenly as a result of a car accident and my mother lost what was left of her reason.

I never met my father's first wife—even my mother never saw her—and so I don't know why her memory wrings my heart. I don't know where she is buried, nor do I recall any of her children ever visiting her. Neither my father nor any of her children ever talked about her. But I used to hear my paternal uncle's wife telling my mother her story and recounting how she had spent her two final years in isolation far from her children in a hospital in the capital, a long way away from the town where we lived.

At an early age I read the story of the Prophet Muhammad's marriage to one of his wives and how he was on the point of going to bed with her when he discovered white marks on the skin of her abdomen and dismissed her. In my young mind this story of the Prophet's marriage became connected with my father's abandonment of his ailing wife, who died alone after two years during which she never saw her children. I harbored feelings of hatred toward my father, though not toward the Prophet, because—you see—the ogre had taken me prisoner, as well.

The boulders continue to descend centuries after Muhammad's death. It is now Saudi sheikhs who bombard us every day with hundreds of fatwas. A large number of Koranic verses deal with women, yet not one of them moderates the severity of the crisis caused by the verses and stories we've talked about already. One verse reads: "Your women are your fields: go, then, into your fields as you please" (2:223). According to Al-Jalalayn's commentary on the Koran,* this expression means that woman is where you plant your children and do so, as you please. According to this same commentary this verse means that a man can sow his sperm in any position he may wish the woman to assume during the "planting process." A woman, therefore, is like

---

* Al-Jalalayn is one of the most significant *tafsirs* (commentary) for the study of the Koran.

the land—the dirt—while the man is the farmer who plows that land and casts his seed into it. The dirt cannot protest as the farmer furrows it, nor can it determine the time or place of planting. The whole operation takes place under the man's control and is carried out in accordance with his wishes. Can the dirt protest? Can the dirt decide how it is plowed and planted? For fourteen centuries Muslim women have been the dirt of Islam that Muslim men have trod on and "planted" in their role as the farmer.

A woman may not step beyond the limitations of her role while the man permits no infringement of his. This stilted relationship has created untold generations born without the benefit of a loving relationship between the men and women who created them. A healthy and loving relationship between a man and a woman in no way resembles the relationship between a farmer and his land. Relationships that are not based on an equal respect for each other's feelings cannot produce a generation sound in mind, spirit, and emotion. A woman is not just a plot of land for a man to cleave with his plow. A woman is a human being with a mind, a soul, and feelings and a man should not be modeled as a sort of farmer who uses a woman as he pleases.

What kind of deity is it whose limited powers of imagination dictates that the relationship between a man and a woman should be similar to that between a farmer and his land? For me, that deity is nothing but a failed poet whose verses we can well do without. That deity is nothing but a puny village ogre who puts men and women on unequal footing as far as their rights and obligations are concerned. Why? The men of the Arabian Desert created their ogre as a way of dealing with their fears. And so this ogre rejected equality in order to punish women for being one of the sources of his fear of failure and disgrace.

When I began to learn to read, the Koran was the first book I opened. I can never remember anyone explaining these verses to me in a more merciful and tolerant way than I understand them today. Today most Muslims attack me unmercifully. They accuse me of picking out from the Koran those verses which serve my purposes, just as I would pick the best cherries out of a boxful. Naturally, I like this simile, and cannot see anything in it that reflects badly on my reliability. The box that God reveals is not supposed to have any spoiled cherries in it. If God does exist, then the most basic moral principle is that this God should be utter perfection. As far as I am concerned, any impairment of perfection diminishes the authenticity of a God. A God who subjugates women in the ugliest ways possible cannot possibly possess the necessary quality of perfection. If I can pick out spoiled cherries from a box that is supposed to have come down from God, then I have every right to cause you to doubt the authenticity of that God.

The status of women in Muslim countries is a human catastrophe that the world has ignored for centuries and for which it is now paying a high price for ignoring. An oppressed and subjugated woman cannot give birth to an emotionally and mentally well-balanced man. The invisible Muslim woman has been and continues to be the hen who incubates the eggs of terrorism and provides them with the necessary warmth to hatch the terrorists.

The woman who stands before the television camera and tells the world, "Three of my sons were martyrs and I hope the fourth becomes one, too," is a woman who has been deprived of her motherhood. And when she continues, "My sons are now cele- brating their marriage with their virgins in paradise," we must conclude that she has been deprived of sense and conscience, too! Who has deprived this woman of her motherhood, her mind, and her conscience? People, both men and women, fall into the trap laid for them by those who educate them in the first years of their lives. People are what they are told to be. A person takes on an identity and defines the characteristics of that identity in accordance with the beliefs that prevail in the environment into which he or she has been born. Unconsciously he or she tries to establish the validity of this identity and these characteristics.

It is difficult, if not impossible, to change one's beliefs about oneself later in life, especially if one continues to live in the environment that helped form those beliefs. I read of a curious experiment conducted by a psychologist who adopted a female chimpanzee from the moment she was born and took her to live at home with his wife and children as one of the family. The chimpanzee did the same things that the rest of the fam- ily did, and everyone treated her as if she was one of them. When she reached maturity, the psychologist gave her a collec- tion of pictures and asked her to classify them into two groups, the first of which would contain only pictures of nonhumans— such as a book, a cap, a flower, or a bird—while the second would contain pictures of human beings. The pictures the psychologist gave her included one of the chimp herself. The chimpanzee began to sort through the pictures, and she placed the photograph of herself in the group that contained pictures of human beings, for she considered herself to be human. Why? Because she had been treated like a human being since she was born. Women in Muslim countries have fallen into the same trap as that chimpanzee, and can no longer perceive themselves other than as society treats them: as inferior to men and lacking men's mental capacities. They have become convinced that they are inferior beings, and even begin to defend their classification as such.

Muslim education has stunted women to the point of depriving them of their mind and their conscience. This education has had a profound effect on the minds of Muslim men and women alike. It is no longer just men who are responsible for the situation women are in; women themselves have begun to defend the situation. Women have seen themselves relegated to the status of men's animals. They accepted this status and can now no longer escape it.

The Koranic verses and prophetic traditions we've talked about—together with the fatwas, interpretations, and exegeses that accrued to them—were enough to distort women's self-image and persuade them that this distorted image was sacred. Islam views women as defective beings, and, because of the education they have received, women have become convinced of their defectiveness and have indeed sanctified that defectiveness as divine decree. The problem is no longer simply one of Islamic education. It is being perpetuated by women who defend this education. No situation can be changed unless those living within it are aware of its shortcomings and strive for change.

A worm lives out its life glued to the ground, frequently crushed underfoot. As it is unaware of the reality it lives in, it does not rebel. Women in Muslim countries live like worms, trampled under men's feet. They believe that they were created to follow that way of life, and so cannot be expected to reject it.

The prophetic traditions I have quoted stigmatized women as intellectually and morally defective. Muhammad in a hadith told his followers: "Oh ye women, you are the majority of those who dwell in hell, for when you receive you express no thanks, when afflicted you show no patience, and when I keep aloof from you, you complain." Just imagine for a moment how it must feel to hear this over and over again, having it drummed into your head until it becomes part of your very being. According to Muslim belief, women are incapable of gratitude or patience and like to grumble and complain. What kind of woman is this brainwashed female who agrees to descend to the level of these accusations?

Women in Islam have not just become the hostages of their own debilitating beliefs about themselves. They are also at men's beck and call and, thus, their hostages, as well. Muhammad said in another hadith: "A woman must not feed anyone without her husband's permission, unless the food is about to spoil. If she feeds anyone with his consent, her recompense is the same as his, but if she feeds anyone without his permission, he receives the recompense, while she will bear the responsibility for the sin." What kind of woman is this brainwashed female who does not have the right to dispose of so much as a loaf of bread in her own home, and who, if she gives it to a destitute person with her husband's permission, only then gets her recompense from his God? These teachings have not just helped to canonize women's bondage, they have enshrined male arrogance.

The Muslim male is conceited. His ogre has appointed him as his deputy and has conferred absolute power upon him. This power knows no bounds and has no respect for women's intelligence or emotions. Even where something as private and personal as having sex with one's spouse is concerned, Islam gives women no choice in the matter. Muhammad: says in another hadith "If a man summons his wife to his bed and she refuses, the angels will curse her until the morning." Who is this God who asks his angels to devote their attention to cursing women who refuse to go to bed with their husbands? Is he not an ogre? When there is a conflict between obeying her husband and obeying God, a woman owes her first obedience to her husband. This means that she is not allowed to fast or pray unless her husband agrees, as laid down by the words of the Prophet of Islam in a hadith: "A woman shall neither fast nor pray without her husband's authorization."

Muslim women live as men's slaves and will remain so until they release themselves from this mistaken conviction. Can you imagine how enslaved a woman must be if she believes this hadith from her Prophet: "A man has the right to expect his wife, if his nose runs with blood, mucus or pus, to lick it up with her tongue." Can you imagine the conceit of a man who believes that his God has entitled him to such a position that his wife must lick up the filth that comes out of his nose?

During my last visit to Syria in 2005, a childhood friend of mine invited me to lunch at her home in a Damascus suburb. Around the table with me were my friend and her family and a friend of hers called Halima. My friend's friend was a woman in her forties. The story of her life was eloquently and clearly expressed in her face, a face filled with sorrow. "When I heard you'd been invited to Reema's," she said, "I called her and asked her to arrange for me to meet you at any cost. I've read you, and I know perfectly well who you are and what you can and can't do. I don't want anything from you. I ask only that you listen to my story because no one else here seems to believe that I have a story worth telling."

And so, she told me her story, one that has unfortunately become part of the social fabric of the place, a story also heard in other cultures of a woman who is used by a man; but one that, here, has a different Koranic twist to it. It's a story that people have grown used to hearing and no longer, unfortunately, find a cause for concern. . . .

Halima has three children. She spent her childhood and early youth in the house of her father, who never accorded her a single day's respect either as a woman or a human being. She escaped into marriage to a man named Omar while still an adolescent, seeking refuge from a bad situation in one that turned out to be even worse. After her marriage, Omar came home drunk every night and beat her. She became accustomed to these daily beatings, just as he was accustomed to drinking.

But Halima is no ordinary woman. She is a teacher, poised yet noticeably wary. Her tragedy came to a head when her drunken husband began to put pressure on her to arrange a bank loan for him on the strength of her salary to pay off his accumulated debts, to creditors whose patience was running out. Halima tried to find out whether or not what Omar said was true, in order to discover the names of his creditors and pay off the debt herself so that her husband would have no need of the loan—but without success.

Women, in Omar's view, were supposed to carry out their husband's orders without protest and had no right to interfere in a man's affairs. He used to tell her from time to time, over the sound of his belt ripping into her body, "You damned woman, have you forgotten the words of God's Prophet—may God bless him and grant him salvation: 'If I had ordered any-one to bow down to anyone [other than God], I would have ordered a woman to bow down before her husband because of his rights over her.' I haven't ordered you to kneel down in front of me, but I am ordering you to take out a loan on the strength of your salary!" Halima secured the loan and Omar pocketed the money, leaving the house reassured that Halima had obeyed her Prophet and her husband, earning the ap-proval of her Lord.

After Omar had taken Halima's money, he was repeatedly and inexplicably absent from home and Halima became suspi-cious. One morning their neighbor, Salim, knocked at their door. "How are you, Halima? Listen, there's something I want to tell you. Before Omar leaves home tomorrow morning, make sure he hasn't got his passport in his pocket." Then he turned on his heel and hurried away before Halima could ask why.

After beating Halima into exhaustion, Omar left the house that morning and did not return. Five months earlier, Omar had met a Moroccan dancer in a Damascus nightclub and had formed what he described as a "fraternal" relationship with her. When the dancer's contract came to an end and she went back to her own country he kept in contact with her to "keep a brotherly eye on her and make sure she's all right." Once Omar got ahold of the loan money, he bought a ticket to Morocco leaving Halima and their children alone and in debt. Halima shared her income with the bank to pay the debt, but what re-mained was not enough to feed her children.

But the story didn't stop there. Her entire salary evaporated when she discovered that the telephone bill amounted to 70,000 Syrian pounds (the average sum a Syrian earns in ten months), all of which had been spent on Omar's telephone calls to Morocco to set his mind at rest as to the well-being of his "sister." Halima could have left the bill unpaid, as she had no need of a phone and did not care if the telephone company cut her off. The drama, however, took another twist that favored another man in Halima's life: The phone bill was registered in her father's name. Instead of helping his daughter, Halima's father made her promise to pay the bill before he would agree to have the line reinstalled in her home.

The only bright spot for Halima was when the Damascus telephone company took pity on her and agreed to take a share of her monthly salary as well, creating an even smaller amount of money with which she was to feed her children. Halima continues to work at her day job at the school to satisfy the creditors' demands. When the school day is over, she runs from house to house giving private lessons to students so that she can perhaps manage to feed three hungry mouths. My heart bled for her as I saw her beautiful eyes fill with tears. I patted her shoulder, while a voice inside me murmured, "Don't be sad, Halima. You've paid an exorbitant price, but you've pleased your God and his Prophet. That's the way of the world, whose pleasures are fleeting. Patience, Halima, paradise is waiting!" I didn't tell her. Nothing I could have told her. All that she wanted from me was to listen to her story.

Halima gave me a present. When I opened it I found inside two Syrian-made cotton shirts. I was delighted by her gift, a beautiful memento of my homeland and testimony to the tragedy of a woman I had met and before whose tears I had been helpless. It is my custom, when I receive a gift from someone dear to me, to inscribe the present with the giver's name and the date on which it was presented, together with a sentence reminding me of the circumstances in which it was given. I folded one of the shirts and put it away for safekeeping with the inscription: HALIMA, SYRIA, 12 APRIL 2005, but I could find no sentence which summarized the situation better than Eleanor Roosevelt's remark: "No one can put you down without your consent."

Halima's husband had humiliated and diminished her, but he had done it with her consent. Along with the arrogance and tyranny which her husband's education nurtured in him as a Muslim male, there is another more powerful thing responsible for Halima's tragedy: her acceptance of the slave role dictated to her by her husband's Prophet. It is Halima who needs to be re-educated. Omar's reeducation, if he ever leaves his Moroccan dancer to rejoin his wife, will follow as an inevitable consequence of a change in her. We cannot release Omar from his arrogance as long as he reads and believes the hadith: "A man has the right to expect his wife, if his nose runs with blood, mucus or pus, to lick it up with her tongue." But we can give Halima back her power by amending her self-image for her. If that can happen, and if she can shed the role of slave, which has been handed down to her through the centuries, she will tell Omar to clean up his own filth instead of expecting her to lick it up for him.

A woman like Halima, however, cannot be persuaded to change her situation unless she has the opportunity to compare it with that of others. This is precisely what happens when a Muslim woman emigrates to a Western country where women's rights are assured. In most cases she will try to change her situation as a result of what she observes in her new surroundings. However, Muslim women who have built Westernized lives for themselves in Western countries and enjoy the same rights as women in their adopted society are not always prepared to acknowledge what their new societies have done for them. On the contrary, they boast that the rights they now enjoy are no different from those which Islam granted them. Sometimes they go so far as to claim that the West uses women only for sex and places no value on her humanity. I have gotten into conversations with Muslim women now living in America who enjoy the same rights as American women do. Most of them insisted that their lives in America were no different from their lives in their homeland. This bizarre statement, which I was stunned by over and over again, always made me shake my head and wonder if, as they say, these women and I lived on different planets.

On my way from New Jersey to Pennsylvania, I got off at Trenton to change trains and sat in the station hall with the other passengers, waiting for the next train to arrive. To my right was a trolley piled with almonds and nuts, and beside it stood a broad-shouldered dark-skinned man of medium height whom I took at first glance for a Native American. He left his trolley, took two steps forward, and declaimed the call to prayer in Arabic: "God is great. God is great. The time of prayer has come. The time of prayer has come."

I was pleased to hear someone speaking my native language, so I went over to have a word with him. Summoning my energies, I said, *"Al-salamu 'aleikum!"* ("Peace be upon you!")

He responded in astonishment, *"Wa'aleikum al-salam!"* ("And on you be peace!")

I asked him in English, "Do you speak Arabic?"

He replied, "I read Arabic. It's the language of my Koran."

"And do you understand it?"

He replied evasively, "Yes . . . yes. Do you want to enter Islam?"

"But I am a Muslim," I told him.

His eyes blazed like live coals: "You are not a Muslim, and you don't belong in Islam!"

His response shocked me, and I asked him, "Who are you to judge me?"

In a grinding voice he continued rudely, "Are you crazy? A Muslim woman covers her head, keeps to the house, and raises her children. She doesn't go wandering around among men in the land of the unbelievers! Fear God, go home, and take care of your children!"

I looked him in the face and shouted at him, "Yes, I am crazy, because I expected something good from a religious fanatic. You fool! If your women had brought up your children properly, Pakistan would be the Switzerland of Islam and you wouldn't have ended up on the West's doorstep like beggars." Then I left him, muttering to myself in Arabic, the language he couldn't read, didn't understand, and just repeated, parrot-like. I said, "It's not your stupidity that upsets me. I feel sorry for America which allows fools like you to pollute it."

I have no hopes for Muslims, men or women, who live in the West. They are, quite simply, hypocrites. They are trying to have the best of both worlds. They live and enjoy the carefree Western lifestyle to the full while at the same time pretending to their relatives back home that they devoutly observe the teachings of Islam and try to spread and apply them in the West.

In 2003, on my first visit to Syria since my emigration, I met a Syrian lady who was living in America and whose visit to Syria happened to coincide with mine. We met at a social gathering, and, before we had made each other's acquaintance, I heard her telling a group of women, "A number of scholars and psychologists in the United States have found a way of treating mood disorders with recitation from the Holy Koran." She was showered with questions from every side and began, without qualification, to describe to them what life in America was like; how people had lost their spirituality and were now ruled by their greed and their dependence on material things, how they were searching for a meaning in life, and had begun to find it in the teachings of Islam. Muslims of this kind present a danger not only in the United States, but also in their countries of origin.

People in Islamic countries are experiencing a terrible psychological struggle. They are dazzled by what they see and hear of the West and discontented with their situation in their homeland. However, at the same time, influenced by what they have heard from those who have already gone to live in Western countries, they are confused, and waver between their own culture, which has worn them out, and Western culture, which is condemned by those Muslims who live under its flag. When I joined in the discussion and asked her about her decision to live in American society and why she and her three children did not come back to live in her own "spiritual" society, she stared at me disapprovingly and indicated to me tersely that, though she wanted to return in the near future, the political and economic situation in her homeland prevented her from doing so at present.

I broke off the conversation at that point, convinced of the impossibility of reaching any logical conclusion with her. I have witnessed many scenes and heard many stories that embody this struggle, the most amusing of which I still remember from a number of years ago. President Gaddafi had expelled a group of young Palestinians from Libya in protest against the Oslo Accords between the Palestinian and Israeli governments. The Palestinians were gathered at the border between Libya and Egypt waiting for the United Nations to take pity on them and solve their problem. In the scene I remember, a group of Palestinians were protesting against Gaddafi's decision by burning the American flag. One of them brandished the burning flag. The logo on his T-shirt read CHICAGO BULLS.

Women in Muslim countries, isolated from the hypocrisy of their sisters who live in the West, can only observe what Western women have accomplished when they exercised their rights and freedoms and received the education that enlightened their minds. The woman in the Muslim country is forced to recognize that Western culture is the fruit of men and women working together equally and to acknowledge that societies which demean and oppress half their members will not be able to succeed on any level nor make any kind of progress at all. Releasing these women from their ignorance is the key to the doors that the teachings of Islam have closed firmly in their faces. Only when we have managed to open these doors will we have taken the first step toward stamping out Islamic terrorism.

When Muslim women realize the difference between decision

and choice they will be able to respect their freedom rather than glorify their slavery. When we broach the subject of the head covering, which has kept Muslim women hidden from the entire world and has erected an iron barrier between men and women who live in the same society, these women protest that covering their heads is a decision they themselves have taken and that the rest of the world has to respect it. It may be their decision, but it is certainly not their choice. It is fear which binds women in Arab countries to these teachings.

The Prophet Muhammad told his cousin Ali in a hadith: "On the night the angel took me up into the heavens I passed by hell and saw women suffering all manner of tortures and wept at the sight, so great was their torment. I saw a woman hanging by her hair as her brain boiled, I saw a woman hanging by her breasts and I saw woman with the head of a pig and the body of an ass. I saw a woman in the form of a dog with fire going in through her mouth and emerging from her buttocks as angels beat her head with a stick of flame." Could a Hollywood film director specializing in horror films filled with torture imagine a more terrifying scenario than this? How can a Muslim woman refuse to cover her head when she believes that God will hang her up by her breasts, send fire into her mouth, and bring it out through her backside? She can't and she won't be able to free herself from her head covering until she frees herself from her fear.

When we succeed in releasing that woman from the clutches of her ogre, she will be able to free herself from her fear and then she will take another look at the teachings which have deprived her of her humanity. That is one aspect of the issue. Another aspect is, if covering one's head is a matter of personal decision on the part of Muslim women and the world has to respect this, the question arises: Does Islam respect the decision of women who do not cover their heads? Why can Muslim women walk around the streets of Los Angeles wearing a burka, which covers them from head to toe, while Western women visiting Saudi Arabia have to wear a burka when they go out in public?

Is a Muslim woman who refuses to cover her head treated with respect in Muslim society? Or does she pay a high price for her decision? When I visited Syria two years ago with my American friend Jessica, we sailed to a small island near the Syrian town of Tartus. Together with our guide, a man in his late twenties, we began to explore the island's alleyways, which were crowded with local people and visitors. Jessica remarked: "More women seem to cover their heads here on this island than they do in other Syrian towns."

I turned to the guide and asked him, "Do all the women here on the island cover their heads?"

He answered without hesitation, "Yes, apart from a few prostitutes." His response was nothing more than the reflection of a reality which every woman living in a Muslim society tries to avoid facing. This is one of the most important motives for wearing a hijab. A woman would rather cover her head than be equated with a prostitute.

When I was a fourth-year medical student, at the bus stop one day near the hospital where I was doing my training, I saw two small boys aged about six and eight. Each boy had a small bird in his hand and was plucking out its feathers. The birds were cheeping with pain and struggling to escape. The sight upset me and I went over to the boys and said gently, "Boys, you mustn't do that. Please stop it." The elder boy fixed me with a piercing stare that seemed to penetrate every cell of my body and said vehemently, "There's nothing wrong with plucking a bird. What is wrong is that a woman like you should be walking around off the leash in mixed company without a head covering. Go and bury yourself at home!"

The war on terrorism has to start by protecting Muslim children from teachings that turn them into ogres. Let's give this a bit of thought: The fact that an eight-year-old boy sees right and wrong in these terms is a problem that requires consideration. As far as that boy is concerned, a woman who walks down the street without a head covering is no more worthy of respect than a dog found wandering off the leash. This boy does not need to know anything about the woman, nor does the fact that she is an outstanding medical student concern him as he passes judgment on her and pronounces her a prostitute until she covers her head. The fact that this boy is utterly incapable of any sense of guilt about what he is doing to a small bird is another problem that should arouse our concern.

Muhammad Atta did not become a terrorist overnight. He did not come out of nowhere, nor was he born under a gooseberry bush. When he was eight years old he may well have plucked a little bird's feathers with no sense of guilt and his assumptions regarding a woman without a hijab were no more rational than the small boy's snap judgment of me. He was born into a society whose ethics, teachings, and culture he internalized. In his very early years he must have read the Koranic verse that says: "The punishment of those who wage war against Allah and His Messenger, and strive with might and main for mischief through the land is: execution, or crucifixion, or the cutting off of hands and feet from opposite sides" (5:33). A boy who learns that God cuts off people's hands and feet from opposite sides will not hesitate to pluck a live bird and will be capable, when he grows up, of hijacking a plane carrying "unbelievers" or attacking a tower full of those "unbelievers." That boy will internalize his God and will one day himself become that God. Unfortunately, this indoctrination of the young is spreading.

About two years ago the mosque in Anaheim, Orange County, California, held a children's Koran-memorizing competition, with prizes for the winners. I was stunned. The American government exposes its troops to danger in Iraq and Afghanistan on the grounds of combating terrorism, yet increasingly both the government of the United Sates and the American people turn a blind eye to the fact that American children are imbibing terrorism right here at home. A few weeks after the September terrorist attacks, an Islamic center in Los Angeles contributed a set of books entitled *The Meaning of the Holy Qur'an* to the Los Angeles United School District; however, after an urgent meeting between local Jewish and Muslim leaders, the books were withdrawn from the schools and returned to the Islamic center because some of the teachings they contained offended members of other religious denominations. The *Los Angeles Times* reported the story on February 12, 2002, in an article entitled, "New Version Will Replace Pulled Koran."

The article mentions that Mr. Dafer Dakhil, head of the

Omar Ibn Al Khattab Foundation, e-mailed a reaction to the *Times*, in which he wrote: "The purpose of our gift was to promote a greater understanding of Islam and Muslims at a time when misconceptions and interest about Islam and Muslims are at a peak, and to provide educators and students and opportunity to use Quran alongside the Bible and scriptures of other faiths." Mr. Dakhil had already apologized as follows: "We didn't mean to hurt the feeling or cause discomfort to members of other faiths." Salam Al-Marayati, spokesman for the Muslim Public Affairs Council, explained: "In the interest of good faith and goodwill and being sensitive to people's concerns we agreed that the books should not be used." According to the *Los Angeles Times* article, "Mr. Al-Marayati and other Muslims at the meeting agreed to work with the school officials to find another version of the Quran as soon as possible."

Then, as now, I am filled with questions about what happened: What other version of the Koran do they mean? How would Mr. Al-Marayati interpret for us in his new version the Koranic verse quoted on page 148? Would he tell our children that this verse is no longer applicable in the present day? Ever since then I have followed the news closely, but I have never heard that Mr. Al-Marayati has managed to come up with a different version. Nor do I know how long he meant when he said "as soon as possible." The article says that the meeting took place behind closed doors. Why did the debate not take place publicly? Has Mr. Al-Marayati explained to all Muslims, both here and in Muslim countries, the actual reasons why that version of the book was withdrawn from Los Angeles schools, and has he tried to have it removed from schools throughout the world? What is morally unacceptable in Los Angeles should be morally unacceptable elsewhere, even throughout the Middle East, as morality does not vary with time or place. Why did Mr. Al-Marayati withdraw the book from schools in Los Angeles while allowing others to distribute it as a prize to Muslim children who excelled at memorizing it at the Islamic school affiliated to the mosque in Anaheim?

This is not the only incident, unfortunately, of a Muslim saying one thing to an English-speaking audience and something else entirely to an Arabic-speaking one. In the wake of the September 11th attack, a study event was held at which the main—and only—speaker was a public speaker from the Muslim community. After he had finished speaking, those present began to ask questions, and I asked him: "Doctor, do you believe that the Islamic books we have will contribute to the creation of a peaceable and nonviolent generation?" The speaker was well aware of who I was and of my contributions; he, therefore, replied: "Absolutely not!" implying that Islamic books need to be altered or looked at more carefully. However, when asked by a publisher of a Los Angeles Arabic-language newspaper if it would be okay to quote his answers word for word, he objected. I heard him say, "No, don't do that, but I have no objection to your writing, 'some of these books require re-examination.'" The publisher tried to get the speaker's agreement before printing his views, because deep down he realized that what the speaker had said in a private forum was different from what he was prepared to say publicly.

Why do countries in the West allow Muslims, who live among them, to pretend to be moderates when they speak in

Western languages, but don't criticize them for their radical Islamic views when they address the Muslim world in their native languages? This story is just the tip of an iceberg, which represents the increasing Islamization of the West and, especially, of the United States.

9.

Islam Is a Sealed Flask

ISLAM IS A sealed flask. Its stopper allows no ventilation. In order to safeguard itself and guarantee its continued survival this ideological system holds its people in an iron grip and has created an oppressive and despotic relationship between society and the individual. The individual has no freedom within his society, and no privacy. He has to submit to his society and has been deprived of his ability to express his opinion, especially when that opinion is not the prevailing one. Islam has deprived its followers of the most basic form of freedom—the freedom to express oneself. And it has killed their desire to enjoy this freedom. In order to ensure its control over the individual, it has interfered in all aspects of his life, large and small, and has planned it out for him in every particular. It micromanages his every activity and regulates the most private moments of his life—to the point of commanding him to put his left foot before his right when he gets into the bath.*

Relationships between individuals within this society are

---

*It's an Islamic tradition that you enter a room with your right foot except for the bathroom, because it's considered to be a "dirty place."

organized in such as way as to make each member of it simultaneously a master and a slave. In relationships with those weaker than himself he is a master; when the other person is stronger, he is the slave. The nature of the relationship between God and Man in Islam is no different from the relationship between the ruler and his subjects, between man and wife, between father and son, and between master and slave. It is an oppressive relationship that does not permit any straying outside the boundaries of what the supreme authority has permitted. Woman is the property of Man, a child is the property of his father, a slave is the property of his master, and a laborer is the property of his employer. All of these are the property of the ruler, who governs by divine decree.

As long as the slave continues to acknowledge the rights of his master and refuses to violate their sanctity, this oppressive pecking order will survive and be perpetuated. All social institutions in Muslim society are founded on oppressive proprietary relationships. Muslim society has been a slave society since it came into being and has remained so ever since. A researcher or human-rights activist has only to live in a Muslim society to be convinced of the truth of this. If he does so, he will fully experience the nature of the relationships that create the fabric of that society. When you watch how people in Muslim society relate to one another—even in a one-on-one relationship—you see a master and a slave. Simple observation will enable you to observe what takes place between the two parties.

The human mind is programmed to feel inferiority or mastery in accordance with the status of each party. When two parties meet, each of them recognizes in some imperceptible way which of them is the stronger. The weaker party discards all his cards, while the stronger takes control and begins to impose his conditions. In Muslim society very few relationships are founded upon mutual respect. Even at the level of personal friendship, each party is well aware of the other's weaknesses and strengths. When two people meet, each recognizes by a simple process of calculation which of them is the stronger, and each will naturally incline to play the role of either the master or the slave.

I even saw the truth of this when I watched people's behavior at social gatherings. So-and-so meets So-and-so, and each of them knows within a few minutes of meeting what the other does, who his family is, how well off he is, and what religious denomination or tribe he belongs to. This initial encounter defines how each of them will behave toward the other. However small the difference between the two parties may be, one will always dominate while the other submits, with no half measures.

A person may be a master in one relationship and a slave in another. The strength of the other party in the relationship determines which of the two roles he plays. One of my relatives used to work as an aide to a high-ranking officer in Syrian intelligence. When I went to visit him at his office I was able to observe his behavior firsthand. Within the space of several minutes I saw him play the role of supreme master and abject slave. When his telephone rang and he realized that his superior officer was on the line, he rose to his feet and signaled to the other people in his office to be quiet. He started to sweat as he said, "Yes, sir. You give the orders and I am your faithful servant. I shall carry out your orders to the letter and apprise you meticulously of all the

details." After he put down the phone he turned to a man standing at the office door and shouted at him: "Listen, you son of a
whore, I'm sending you on an assignment, and you'll carry it out
to the letter. If you don't, it'll be a black day for you!" The man
replied, "Yes sir! You give the orders and I am your faithful servant." While one might imagine such an incident taking place in
an intelligence apparatus anywhere in the world, it really does
embody the reality of Muslim societies. Anyone who reads Muslim history as related by Arab sources becomes aware of the oppressive nature of relationships between any two parties within
that society.

In the months following the American army's entry into Iraq
I followed news reports in both the American and Arabic press.
In one of the reports on the situation in Iraq I read an interview
in the *Los Angeles Times* with an American soldier. "I can't understand the Iraqis at all," he said in the article. "People come to
apply for a job. I do my best to help them stand in line, but they
crowd round in a disorganized manner and won't follow instructions. But when an Iraqi soldier comes along and hits them
with his stick, they wait their turn properly. I can't understand
the way they think! The only thing they seem to understand is
the use of force." Yes, indeed, every interaction requires a strong
party and a weak one to regulate the relationship.

When you speak calmly to a Muslim, he perceives you as being weak. The American saying "speak softly and carry a big
stick," is, unfortunately, of no use when dealing with Muslims. It
would be more appropriate to say (until we can change this way
of thinking), "speak forcefully and carry a big stick"; otherwise
you will be the weaker party and the loser. Democracy cannot
spread in societies like these until the people who live in them

have been reeducated, for they cannot function unless they are playing the role of the master or the slave. People in these societies, who are always prepared to assume one role or the other, have to learn how to function as human beings without having to enslave themselves or anybody else. They have to learn that in a proper relationship each party respects the other, recognizes the other's rights and responsibilities, refrains from infringing upon the other's rights, and does not try to avoid the claims of mutual responsibility.

Muhammad, to impose his authority, sowed unease in the hearts of his followers by linking obedience to God with obedience to himself. Then he added a third party to this "holy duality" in the form of the ruler, through whom he could control the rest of his flock.

Muhammad understood that the ruler was the link between himself and the populace, and so concentrated on the need to obey the ruler, saying in a hadith: "Whosoever obeys me obeys God, and he who obeys my emir obeys me. Whosoever disobeys me disobeys God, and he who disobeys my emir disobeys me." In confirmation of this, a verse rolled down from the mountaintop, as follows: "Obey Allah and the Apostle and those in authority among you" (4:59) "Those in authority among you" means, according to works of Koranic exegesis, "your rulers."

In order to ensure that Muslims would obey their rulers implicitly and without reservation, Muhammad told them in a hadith: "Obey your emir even if he flogs you and takes your property." Fearing that some Muslims would rebel against such unquestioning obedience, he justified it by saying in another hadith: "If a ruler passes judgment after profound consideration and his decision is the right one, he is rewarded twice. If he passes judgment after profound consideration and his decision turns out to be the wrong one, he receives a single recompense."

Muhammad was trying to persuade Muslims that the ruler spent time in deliberation and reached a decision only after profound thought. His decision might be right or wrong, but, whichever it was, God would reward him, because he had reached the decision he firmly believed best served Muslim interests. When he made the right decision, God recompensed him doubly, and when he made the wrong one, he gave him a single recompense.

When Saddam Hussein scorched the Kurds of northern Iraq with chemicals and annihilated the Shia in the south, he committed no crime under Muslim religious law. According to the Sharia, he, as ruler, reflected at length before reaching the decision to burn and exterminate. His only punishment under Muhammad's law was that God recompensed him only once. That is, if he made the wrong decision—but who can tell? Perhaps it was in the interests of Islam and the Muslims to burn and exterminate Iraq's Kurds. Never in the history of Islam has a Muslim cleric protested against the actions of a Muslim ruler, because of the total belief that obedience to the ruler is an extension of obedience toward God and his Prophet. There is only one exception to this: A Muslim cleric of one denomination may protest against the actions of a ruler who belongs to a different one.

How can a Muslim escape the grasp of his ruler when he is completely convinced of the necessity of obeying him? How can he protest against this obedience, which represents obedience to his Prophet and therefore also to his God? He cannot.

Islam is indeed a despotic regime. It has been so since its inception, and remains so today.

Is there a relationship more representative of the ugliest forms of slavery than that between a ruler and a populace whom he flogs and whose money he steals while they themselves have no right to protest against his behavior? The ruler acts by divine decree, and the people obey him by divine decree. The United States did not create the dictatorships in the Muslim world. I have no doubt that it supported some of the most despotic Muslim regimes, such as that of Saddam Hussein, but it did not give birth to him. Saddam Hussein was conceived in the womb of Islamic culture. He was sired by the Muslim people, which creates its leaders in accordance with Muslim religious law and in accordance with the master they require. No ruler anywhere in the world can oppress his people unless that population is educationally, culturally, mentally, and psychologically prepared to be oppressed. In the Muslim home oppression starts as soon as a child first sees the light of day, and the acculturation process continues throughout life to the point that, should the subject find himself confronted with his ruler, he will be overwhelmed to the point of being utterly unable to function.

In Islam, children are property, not a responsibility. Islam defines the relationship between child and parents and emphasizes the necessity for blind obedience to them.

A boy's relationship with his father reflects upon his relationship with all other adults in his environment. He takes this relationship with him from his home into the street, the mosque, his school, and all other institutions in his society and uses it to construct similar relationships in which he regards himself as obliged to obey anyone older or more important than himself.

The child is the slave of his teacher, his neighbor, and his relatives—and when he grows up he is the slave of his boss and every other authority figure in his environment. Consciously and unconsciously he accepts this slavery, which represents obedience to God, his Prophet, and those who have authority over him. A boy leaves home and goes to school oppressed and deprived of the basic ability to protest, or just say "no." At school he hears every day what he has heard at home: that God has decreed that parents and those in authority must be obeyed, and he behaves as he has learned to do at home. Everything he learns is instilled in him in a manner that brooks no question that may contain even the hint of a threat to the legitimacy of that obedience. Islam concerns itself with fathers' responsibility for their sons only where religious obligations and duties are concerned. Muhammad said in a hadith: "Teach your children to pray at the age of seven and beat them if they don't at the age of ten."

Here, once again, we see the oppressive relationship manifesting itself even between Man and God: If Man does not pray voluntarily, he has to be forced to do so! I have a Muslim Iranian friend who lives here in the United States. He suffers from severe depression and a number of other psychological disorders which none of the currently available treatments can relieve. He once discussed these issues with me and he told me: "My childhood still haunts me. When I was a boy of seven, my father used to wake me at five in the morning for the dawn prayer. We had no bathroom, and he used to force me to go outside in subzero temperatures to perform the ritual ablution in the waters of the well near our home. I remember that once I just dipped my arms into the pail of water I had drawn up from the bottom of the well then ran toward the house in an attempt to convince my father that I had washed as prescribed, but he was watching me from the window. He took his leather belt and beat me unmercifully while my mother looked on from afar and cried, because I was screaming so loudly."

My Iranian friend continued: "I hate God more than I hate my father. My father and I are both victims of that criminal called Allah."

Saddam Hussein was his victim, too.

Was Saddam Hussein not completely convinced that he represented God and his Prophet on earth? Did he not believe that the Kurds and the Shia should be crushed because they had not obeyed him, even though God had ordered them to obey their ruler? Why should we put Saddam Hussein on trial before trying that "God"? Why should Saddam suffer in jail while that "God" sits at liberty on the mountaintop in our village waiting to pounce on his next victim? The United States was accused by Muslims of supporting dictatorships in their countries, and to defend their ground and relinquish their guilt America decided to bring down Saddam Hussein's throne. But though the throne has gone, the objective has not been attained, and the Iraqi people are still embroiled in the nightmare of that "God," who orders them to obey their leaders. America miscalculated, and the inescapable question now is: Can it do anything to remedy the political situation?

The answer is not only that America can, but that it must! I am not talking about the political or military aspects here—I am no politician and know nothing of military constraints. But

I firmly believe that it is in America's interests to redress the balance, at least insofar as the demands of behavioral science and mental health are concerned. If it was America's intention to use its war in Iraq to help spread democracy throughout the Arab world, in order to make amends for having supported dictatorships there, we have to ask the following question: How can we hope to impose democracy on people who have believed for the past fourteen centuries that they are obliged by divine decree to obey their rulers, even when these rulers persistently violate their rights? What we see happening in Iraq, unfortunately, provides us with the answer to this question.

For this crisis does not involve a democratic leader. It is the crisis of a nation and of a religious law whose decrees and teachings have permeated the convolutions of the brain and stamped themselves on the genes of the people of that nation. Another question raises itself here: What is the solution, and what choices does America have in its war in Iraq? The answer, without going into detail, is, quite simple: The only option it has is to strip this ogre of its power! Free the clergy of their ogre, free the ruler of the clergy, free men of their ruler, free women of men, free the slave of his master—in short, free the people of their fear! What freedom can a man who worships an ogre ever have? If the United States wants to free Muslims from the dictatorship of their rulers, it must first of all strive to free them from the dictatorship of their ogre.

In order to free Muslims from their fears it will take more than any country's army and naval fleets. It's going to require the services of its medical and scientific laboratories and of its experts on behavioral science, social psychology, and sociology. Everyone from popular psychologists like Dr. Wayne Dyer and

Dr. Phil McGraw to researchers doing work in colleges and universities will have to be enlisted to work on ways of ridding the Muslim people of their ogres. These experts on behavioral science and psychology will have, in their proposals, to strive for scientific and ethical accuracy, throwing political correctness out the window.

Many psychologists and behavioral science experts in the United States have studied how children's behavior is affected by the violence they see on television, and have found a correlation between the two. However, from my close observation of what many of them choose to study, I have found they don't have the same desire to investigate the nature of the relationship between violence and reading matter.

Whatever has been said in the past and will be said in the future about the role of television in shaping a person's convictions, I do not believe that it has played or ever will play as important a role as books do. And this is even truer when the book in question is a religious one, and when it is the sole source of knowledge for people who are bedazzled by reading it. There can be no doubt that violence among children in America, or any other Western society, is an extremely dangerous phenomenon and one worthy of study and the most serious consideration. But in no society in which it occurs does it constitute a danger comparable to that presented by Islamic terrorism. America and the whole civilized world will have to pay greater attention to this phenomenon by studying the reasons behind it and ways to deal with it, so as to protect the world, including Muslims themselves.

The Arab heritage has to be acquired from Arab books. I

say "Arab," not "Muslim," so as to ensure that the student will read the primary sources of Islam. For if a researcher deals with Islam as it is presented in Muslim works in languages other than Arabic, he may not succeed in reaching the truth. I say this even though I have never read such books myself, but my close acquaintance with many non-Arab Muslims and my reading of English translations of the Koran have led me to form this conviction. My life in the United States has brought me into professional and social contact with many Muslims who are not Arabs, and these relationships have enabled me to delve deeply into their understanding of Islam and the extent of their knowledge of its teachings. I emerged convinced that there is a great deal of difference between Arab and non-Arab Muslims.

The Koran is an Arabic book, and Islam forbade its translation into any other language. This means that many non-Arabic-speaking Muslims read the Arabic text without learning to understand the Arabic language. They pronounce the words of the Koran without understanding their meaning; as far as they are concerned it is gibberish. In other cases they read the Koran in Arabic transliterated into their own alphabet, as when an American pronounces the word *madrassa* transliterated into Latin letters without any idea of what the word means in Arabic. Although the Koran has been rendered into other languages, these translations are not completely faithful, and Islam, as I mentioned above, forbids translation of the Koran. Because of this prohibition, translators refer to their work as "An English translation of the meaning of the Koran." Naturally, in their work they try to convey the meaning with the greatest political correctness.

When you read the Koran in English or in any other language, you are reading not a literal translation but, rather, the meaning that the translator wants to impart to the text. Not all Arabic works which deal with Muhammad's life, conduct, and thought have been translated into the languages spoken by non-Arab Muslims, and what translations do exist are not faithful to the original. The works have been abridged, and the translations have been adapted to conform to what the translator considers morally suitable and acceptable. My work once brought me into contact with three non-Arab Muslim women doctors. Our jobs required us to spend long hours together, and these were interspersed with numerous discussions of Islam and its teachings. I was amazed at the facts I learned in the course of these conversations.

Their knowledge of Islamic teaching was not only limited; it was also very different from my own. They had grown up in a religious environment more fanatical and closed than mine. Non-Arab Muslims pray in Arabic without understanding it. They repeat the words parrot fashion. This is also the case when they read the Koran. I have not the slightest doubt that many Christians who live in the Arab world know a great deal more about Islam than non-Arab Muslims do. What is more, Christians who live in Arab countries are more influenced behaviorally and intellectually by Muslim culture than non-Arab Muslims are.

This explains to a great extent why Islamic terrorism is the product of the Arab heartland. Arab Muslims have a more profound understanding of the Koran, and of the life and sayings of the Prophet Muhammad and what has been written about him. As a result, they have been more exposed to the application of Islamic teachings than have non-Arab Muslims. When an Arabic-speaking Muslim prays, he understands what the prayer means, while a non-Arab Muslim repeats the prayer without understanding it.

A Muslim prays five times a day, and on each occasion he recites the Fatiha, the first verse of the Koran, a number of times. This verse describes Christians as "those who have gone astray" and Jews as "those who have incurred Your wrath." We see from this that Muslims execrate Christians and Jews a number of times in the course of a single prayer, which they repeat five times a day. Non-Arab Muslims are unaware that they are cursing the Christians and the Jews, because they pray in Arabic without understanding what they are saying. This means that the quantity of hatred they absorb from their prayers is less than that absorbed by Arab Muslims, who are aware of what they are saying.

Most non-Arab Muslims I have met in the United States do not know the meaning of this verse that they repeat dozens of times daily in their prayers. However, if you were to ask an Arab boy in the first year of primary school what it meant, he would tell you that the Christians are those who have gone astray while the Jews are those who have incurred God's wrath. Terrorism was born in the Arab world and spread from Saudi Arabia to other Muslim countries with the ideological and financial support of the Arabs. Islamic terrorism is led by Arabs, and those non-Arabs who aspire to leadership are Arab trained.

The Afghans are famous for their saying, "We are at peace only when we are at war." This tendency to strife has penetrated deep into Afghan culture, perhaps because of the tribal nature of Afghan society. But they did not become a source of world

Islamic terrorist activity until they came into disastrous contact with the Arab mujahideen, who brought with them a terrorist philosophy and Arab money. When I discussed this issue with Irshad Manji, author of *The Trouble with Islam Today,* who is of Muslim Indian descent, she did not like the idea and asked me in irritation, "So am I to understand from what you say that non-Arab Muslims are less Islamic than Arab Muslims?"

I replied at once, "No, they are less damaged."

Non-Arab Muslims are not less Islamic than Arab Muslims, if faith and devotion to their religion are the criteria. But if we measure their degree of adherence to Islam by the extent of the mental and psychological damage they have sustained from its teachings, then they are less Islamic. For non-Arab Muslims, generally speaking, do not sink as deeply into the morass of these violent teachings as Arab Muslims do. I am not attempting to deny that there are non-Arab Muslims who are better acquainted with the teachings of Islam and more zealous in their application of them than many Arab Muslims: I am simply trying to make it plain that in the vast majority of cases, Islamic teachings have penetrated the mind of Arab Muslims much more deeply than they have non-Arab Muslims. This fact has to be taken into consideration when formulating a strategy to combat Islamic terrorism. Although Arab Muslims make up no more than 20 percent of the world Muslim population, the reformation of Islam can take place only through them. The reformation of Arab Islam is much more difficult than the reformation of non-Arab Muslims, but it is more important, as they are the source population. This task has to be undertaken before Arab funding "Arab-izes" Islam everywhere in the world as it has in Afghanistan.

I return here to an earlier point: the necessity of studying ter-rorism as a phenomenon in the laboratories of behavioral psy-chology in order to discover the connection between violence and reading matter. Muslim culture, from its Arab beginnings, has canonized violence at all levels. Language is the means by which a culture imposes itself, and members of the community are a linguistic product, and therefore also a cultural one.

I am no expert on linguistics, but I believe that every lan-guage in the world contains expressions and terms sufficient for speakers of that language to understand one another and ex-press themselves. Each language contains positive and negative expressions. Muslim culture uses language in a way which fo-cuses on negative expressions, and so helps to create people with negative attitudes. This is immediately obvious to anyone who reads the Koran or the sayings of the Prophet with the eye of a linguistic researcher.

Let us take a chapter of the Koran, read it, and sift through its phrases. If we take "The Cow," (2:1–286) the longest chapter, what do we find? "They were unbelievers . . . they do not believe . . . great torment . . . they deceive God . . . in their heart is sickness . . . they lie . . . they are the corrupters . . . it is they who are the fools . . . in their tyranny . . . they were not rightly guided . . . God has taken away their light . . . deaf, dumb and blind . . . snatches away their sight . . . bewares the fire . . . break God's covenant . . . refuse to believe in God . . . will shed blood . . . Satan caused them to fall . . . destined for the fire . . . fear Me . . . a great trial from the Lord . . . we drowned Pha-raoh's men . . . you wrong . . . a thunderbolt struck you . . . God's wrath . . . you would have been among the lost . . . your hearts became as hard as rock . . . woe unto those . . . humiliating punishment . . . you are wrongdoers . . . ," etc. Moreover, the word *kill* and its derivatives appears at least twenty-five times in the course of this chapter, which is no more than fifty pages long.

If we disregard the Koran's positive content and the ends to which negative concepts are used, there still remains the linguistic style that predominates in Islamic teachings and which has contributed to the creation of a negative violence-prone personality even in its most positive attitudes. Were an expert on behavioral science to study normal conversation as engaged in by Arab Muslims, he would be surprised by the negative terms in which such conversation is conducted. When an Arab Muslim wants to tell you it's a fine day, he tends to say: "The weather yesterday was worse than it is today." The Koran, to put it mildly, is sadly lacking in positive terms that fall gently upon the ear. For example, in the following Koranic verse from the chapter mentioned above we read: "There is sickness in their hearts which God has increased; they shall be sternly punished for their lying" (2:10). A Muslim may object to my comments, saying: "But in this verse God is trying to demonstrate the importance of truthfulness as a virtue by emphasizing the punishment for lying." My response is this: "Can God not use more positive language to demonstrate the importance of truthfulness?"

Islam forbids usury. If we examine Muhammad's hadiths which confirm this prohibition, what do we find? "He who engages in usury is like one who copulates with his mother." "He who engages in usury is like one who fornicates thirty-three times." "He who engages in usury is like one who swallows

a snake." "He who engages in usury will be raised up as a madman on the day of judgment and will wander confounded like
Satan." I look at the language used here and ask myself how
one can mold a psychologically, morally, and mentally healthy
person with words and expressions like these. Are expressions
such as "copulates with his mother," "fornicates," "swallows a
snake," and "a madman who wanders confounded like Satan"
absolutely necessary in order to deliver the message that usury
is forbidden? Muslims are the inalterable product of what
they read. They are negative people, and their negativism is
reflected in all their attitudes toward life.

On the plane from Amman to New York I passed the time
by leafing through a book I had borrowed from the Arab lady
sitting next to me. The book was entitled *Arab Lovers,* and it
recounted tales of love and passion among the Arabs in the first
centuries of the Muslim era. It was a medium-size book with
big print and I expected it to contain exquisite stories in beautiful language which I would enjoy reading. But I found myself
instead distracted by the frequency with which the phrase "Then
he drew his sword and cut off his rival's head" occurred: I was
surprised to find it appeared twenty-five times in the first sixty
pages. If this is true of a book in which Muslims talk of love
and passion, one can only imagine what happens when they
speak of jihad and of the need to defend God's religion and
uphold his authority! The language of violence and strife has
extended into all areas of life in the Arab Muslim world. An
arithmetic textbook in Saddam Hussein's Iraq posed the following question to third-grade primary-school pupils: "Our
brave soldiers killed 1,500 members of the enemy Iranian forces,
wounded 1,800 others, and took 150 captive. What was the to-

tal extent of enemy losses, including dead, wounded, and captured?" Can arithmetic be taught to third-grade students without the inclusion of a body count?

During the 1973 Arab-Israeli war a Moroccan military unit fought alongside Syrian troops. After the war, rumor spread of the heroism displayed by the Moroccan soldiers; this, however, was merely a lie invented by the Syrians to show their appreciation for the Moroccans' participation in the war. Teachers of classes of all ages were full of praise in their description of their heroism to us pupils. I remember how our religious education teacher elaborated on the heroic exploits of that military unit, and how he insisted that he had seen one of its members carrying a large number of fingers, ears, tongues, and eyes around in his pocket, which had been removed from the bodies of Israeli soldiers killed in the war. We would applaud our teachers happily as they described these "valiant deeds" to us.

Some people accuse Hollywood of bringing more and more violence into our culture. Well, I don't believe that the American film industry centered in Hollywood has ever, in the course of its entire history, succeeded in reproducing so much as a fraction of the violence embodied in the Muslim Arab heritage. There is a difference between the child who sees a violent film on television and the child who hears about it from her teacher or sees that violence enacted all around her in everyday life. All aspects of life in Muslim societies reflect the culture of violence and the negative influence of immersion in a language full of negative words and violent expressions.

Islamic culture invites violence. In most cases it does so openly, in others subtly.

I spoke earlier at length of the background from which Islam emerged: an arid environment with meager resources, daily life shrouded in fears of the unknown, whose inhabitants depended on raiding as a means of survival. The prevailing philosophy in that environment was one of "kill or be killed." Islam adopted the language of that environment, appropriated its negativity and violence then proceeded to legitimize and canonize them.

God, as described in the Koran, possesses the attributes of the men who were the product of that environment. He is highly strung, violent by temperament, lacking in foresight, capricious, fearful of being disobeyed or gainsaid. His fear is reflected in the nature of his commands, and he attacks without mercy. He avenges himself evilly upon those who rebel against him and calls upon people to defend him as if he were unable to defend himself. He promises those who obey him a paradise flowing with rivers and abundant in fruit, and threatens those who revolt against him with a hell where their skin will be flayed off by fire, only to be replaced to be flayed off again. The Koran says: "Those that deny Our revelations We will burn in Hellfire. No sooner will their skins be consumed than We shall give them other skins" (4:56). I once heard a Muslim sheikh explaining the verse to a listener and continuing on: "When they ask you about the mountains. Say: 'My Lord will crush them'" (20:105). I almost tore my hair with fury as I listened to him expatiating upon God's ability to destroy and lay waste, so much so that he seemed to be speaking of Saddam Hussein's devastation of the Kurds and Shias in Iraq.

The Koran does not distinguish between the concepts of "force" and "power." It confuses the two in an odd manner, and God's power manifests itself only as an ability to use force. What is the real difference between the two concepts? A person has power when he can do what needs to be done in a peaceable manner appropriate to the circumstances. He will resort to force only when he is powerless. In other words, power represents peace, while force represents violence.

Arabs who lived in the environment that gave birth to Islam were powerless in the face of the challenges presented by this environment, which threatened their lives and their welfare. Because they felt so helpless they felt a need for forcefulness, and created a god who would fulfill this need. When the Arab male lost his power he felt the need for a forceful god. And so he created a forceful god in the image of his need—but this god was not powerful. A powerful god, like a powerful person, rules his throne and his kingdom in love, peace, compassion, and mercy rather than by killing, inflexibility, and internal strife. A powerful god does not fear that his authority or his mission will be undermined by rebellion, nor does he resort to violence to defend that authority. That is the difference between the Muslim God and the real God, if there is any! The God of Islam uses force, but he has no power.

Let's think about this for a minute: Who is the stronger, Mother Teresa or the ogre at the top of the mountain? Mother Teresa, of course, was the stronger of the two as she was able to accomplish her mission without resorting to force of any kind. But who possesses a greater degree of force, the ogre or Mother Teresa? The ogre, naturally, possesses a greater degree of force for it uses its talons and fangs to devour people. Let us examine the following verse from the Koran: "Prophet, rouse the faithful to arms. If there are twenty steadfast men among you, they shall vanquish two hundred; and if there are a hundred, they shall rout a thousand unbelievers, for they are devoid of understanding" (8:65). When does a God incite his followers to battle? He does that only when he is unable to spread his message by peaceful means. As people internalize their god, they incite others to strife when they lose their power and are unable to accomplish by peaceful methods what has to be done. So force is the only alternative to power! As long as a person has power, he has not need of force. Knowledge, whether religious, scientific, or philosophical, is supposed to arm us with power, not to enable us to use force. Concepts, whether religious or not, can defend themselves, and do not need to be defended by those who believe in them.

As I wrote earlier, among the attributes Islam bestowed upon God are ones such as "The Harmer," "The Avenger," "The Compeller," "The Protector," and "The Imperious." To anyone who examines them, these qualities appear to be of a kind bestowed only on someone who has lost his power and resorted to force to accomplish what he has to do. The Syrian writer Nabil Fayyad says: "The more fragile an idea is, the more terrifying its defenders are." A good concept needs no defenders. The fact that it is necessary guarantees its success and durability. A poor concept cannot defend itself, and finishes up on the garbage heap of history because no one needs it. Ideas, like commodities, compete in the marketplace of history and are subject to the laws of supply and demand. History has proved, in the crush of this competition, that we need only good ideas and that our need for them guarantees their survival and permanence.

A powerless person defends any bad idea that will allow him to exert force, and will risk his life to defend it. You will never be able to persuade such a person of the fragility of his idea unless you help him regain his power. A simple analysis of the reality in which Muslims live suffices to reveal the sterility of Islamic teachings. These teachings have failed to create steadfast, productive, and creative human beings. In the Arab world the clock has stopped, and the calendar is still set at the seventh century c.e. Muslims have lost everything, and have nothing left to identify with except for the teachings to which they cling ever more strongly. The Muslim and the teachings he believes in are chasing each other around a circular track. The teachings pursue him, while he can find nothing to pursue except them. They will lead him to disaster, but his failure will serve only to increase his dependence upon them.

IO.

Islam Is a Closed Market

FROM ITS EARLIEST beginnings Islam has forcibly defended its teachings. It resorted to force because it needed power. It used its might to stamp out any ideas that did not fit into its program, and kept its people firmly locked up in prison. It rejected the principle of excellence and the laws of supply and demand. No merchandise but its own was allowed into its marketplace. The Koran and the life, actions, and sayings of the Prophet Muhammad were the sole source of knowledge and the only basis for legislation. Islam imposed these sources by force and allowed no others to compete with them. With time these other sources lost their authority, as they could no longer compete with the concepts of the new era.

When an idea is no longer appropriate to its time, it loses its excellence and becomes fragile. The more fragile it becomes, the more it deprives its adherents of the ability to keep abreast of the times. Muslims became the hostage of their own doctrinal prison whose teachings had made them feel helpless. This sense of helplessness, in turn, made them all the more dependent on these teachings.

The inhabitants of the Arabian Desert were so intimidated

by their barren environment that they were incapable of any thought of improving or animating it. The fears that beset Muslims pursue them to this day. People cannot solve their problems by using the same ideas that caused the problems in the first place. Fourteen centuries have not convinced Muslims of the barrenness of their teachings, and they still refuse to hold these teachings responsible for their powerlessness and backwardness. These teachings have done nothing to improve their economic, political, social, or moral circumstances, and they remain hostage to the same reality, even though times and places changed.

On the economic front, these teachings did not emphasize the importance of work. The concept of work in Islam was confined to nomadic migration, raiding, booty, and the struggle for survival. Islam promised its followers rivers, fruit, wines, and milk, but it did not encourage them to sink wells, grow fruit, or raise livestock. Its teachings convinced them that life is ephemeral, and that it is valuable only if used to worship God. It deluded them with visions of the hereafter and the gardens of paradise, and they lived on this delusion, waiting for the life to come. They still do.

The Koran says: "This is the Paradise which the righteous have been promised. There shall flow in it rivers of unpolluted water, and rivers of milk forever fresh; rivers of delectable wine and rivers of clearest honey. They shall eat therein of every fruit and receive forgiveness from their Lord. Is this like the lot of those who shall abide in Hell forever and drink scalding water which will tear their bowels?" (47:15). Another verse reads: "The life of this world is but a sport and a pastime. Surely better is the life to come for those that fear Allah" (6:32).

This means that for Muslims life in this world has no value. They are here only temporarily, and have no responsibilities beyond worshipping God so that they can enjoy paradise in the hereafter.

The call to wage war on God's behalf constituted the main part of these responsibilities, as the following Koranic verse makes clear: "Let those who would exchange the life of this world for the hereafter, fight for the cause of Allah; whether they die or conquer, We shall richly reward them" (4:74). Muslims could not conceive of responsibility outside the concept of fighting. They still believe that jihad is the only way to guarantee their entry to paradise in the hereafter. When people bear no responsibility for their actions they cannot admit to having been wrong, and, in consequence, can feel no sense of guilt for their wrongdoings.

Islam considered anything that happened to a Muslim outside the boundaries of the responsibility to fight to be fate, over which he could have no control, and accordingly, no responsibility. Islamic teachings gave Muslims the illusion that their fate was foreordained. It convinced them that every detail of their lives was predestined and that they had no power to influence events. The Koran says: "Say: 'Nothing will befall us except what Allah has ordained'" (9:51). And Muhammad said in a hadith: "If something happens to you, do not say: 'If I had done that, such and such a thing would have happened.' Say, rather: 'Allah has ordained it so, and whatever He pleases He does.'"

This call to submit to whatever fate ordains has helped to foster a dependent attitude and has convinced people that whatever happened in their lives occurred only as part of God's plan and at his command. This attitude enables Muslims to avoid facing reality and also, to a great extent, helps to deprive them of their ability to feel guilt at the wretchedness of that reality. Muslims have never learned to engage in soul searching or to acknowledge where they might have gone wrong. As far as they are concerned, whatever happens is God's will and their faith does not either require them to regret their actions or consider them responsible for any consequences that might ensue.

Let me give you one example: Hassan Nasrallah is a Lebanese Shiite Muslim cleric who has broken the law in his own country, challenged the wishes of its government, and formed his followers into a political party. This may all seem quite reasonable to some people, but I don't believe that there is a person on earth with a grain of sense who can agree with him on the name he has given his party: Hezbollah, which means "the party of God." The name he has chosen for his party reflects the way he thinks. Whether or not we believe in God is immaterial: The important issue here is that a man is claiming to have a monopoly on God and putting himself together with God in the same party. This man does not respect anyone else's right to live, and sets no store by human life. He is convinced that he came into this world to wage war in order to spread the religion of Allah, and that he will enjoy an eternity in paradise whether he kills or is killed. He reckons his gain by the extent of his enemies' losses, but cares nothing for the losses he himself sustains, whether in possessions or human lives.

Nasrallah knew from the outset that he was embarking upon a ruinous war, yet he and his followers led Lebanon to utter disaster in their war against Israel. He emerged from this war with 1,000 people dead, 5,000 wounded, and 1 million displaced, only to announce on the evening of the ceasefire that he had defeated Israel and that he dedicated his victory to Lebanon and the Islamic nation. There you have the Muslim concept of victory.

Nasrallah and his followers managed to kill a hundred Jews, and in his view there is no greater victory than this. The Koran says: "Allah has purchased of the faithful their lives and worldly goods and in return has promised them the Garden. They will fight for His cause, slay and be slain" (9:111) And so it is the Muslim's objective in war either to kill his enemy or to be killed by him, and he considers himself to have won whichever turns out to be the case. If the Muslim kills his enemy he has won, but if his enemy kills him, the Muslim's victory is even greater, as this action on his enemy's part has served only to allow the Muslim to meet his God all the sooner.

Hassan Nasrallah is unable to assume responsibility for what he did, and so cannot feel guilty for what his behavior has brought about. One thousand people dead, 5,000 wounded, and a million left homeless—all these have no importance as compared with the fact that Israel lost a hundred people. This is the philosophy of men who claim to have a monopoly on God and to have formed a party with him. They have dressed God in an army uniform, put a helmet on his head, and pulled him down into the trenches with them so that he will help them wipe out their enemies. Who can compete with such a mentality? Who can fight a man who wishes for his own death more than he wishes for that of others?

When we were young, our elders drummed a saying into us: "We love death as much as our enemy loves life." A man imbued with a culture of death cannot be a human being, because a person's humanity is not complete unless he respects human life and takes action to protect it. A Lebanese woman who had lost two daughters, two sisters, her brother, and both her parents in the recent war between Israel and Hezbollah, was quoted by the *Los Angeles Times* as saying—word for word—"I'm happy now, because they have gone to paradise." War on terrorism is pointless unless the world works together to replace this life-disdaining culture that incites people to sacrifice their lives with a more humane and reasonable alternative.

The concept of responsibility has no place in the customs of Islam. Fourteen centuries later the Muslim nation is at the bottom of the scale of nations, but Muslim men refuse to recognize their responsibility for this regression, which would cause any reasonable person feelings of guilt.

People feel guilty only when they assume their responsibilities and acknowledge that they have failed to perform them properly. The Muslim male is the product of a culture that does not know how to take responsibility and which does not hold him accountable for his failures. If you were to spend a lifetime in his company you would not see him display any feelings of guilt no matter how badly he has failed. In an attempt to avoid facing his failure the Muslim man plays the game of "killer and victim." He is the victim, and the whole world is out to get him!

Since the dawn of Islam Muslims have always divided the world into two—themselves and others—and they continue to do so today. They are reasonable, peaceable, and upstanding believers while everyone else is a thoughtless, wicked, and heretical terrorist. They are the victims, and the others are the killers. But although they have accused the entire world of conspiring to wipe them and their religion out, it is the Jews who have been their scapegoat from Islam's earliest beginnings.

Jew must be one of the words Muslim children hear most frequently before the age of ten. It is also one of the hardest words they hear, as in their imagination it conjures up visions of killing, depravity, lies, and corruption. When two people quarrel, each calls the other a Jew. When one person wishes to express his disdain for another, he will call him a Jew.

When someone wants to describe someone else as ugly, he says he looks like a Jew. We hold the Jews "responsible" for our military failures, our economic backwardness, and our technological dependency. We believe that Jews control the world and that, in consequence, the whole world, dancing to their tune, wants to get rid of us. When I was at primary school the teacher rehearsed us in a play for the national Independence Day celebrations. He cast me in the role of Golda Meir, who was Israel's prime minister at the time. The teacher suggested that I speak in a gruff and uncouth voice and wear disfiguring makeup to make me look convincing in the part as he imagined it.

I felt as if I had been struck by a thunderbolt. My childish mind could not take in what was happening. I felt personally humiliated by the teacher's suggestion, which I found totally unacceptable. I asked myself: I'm to play Golda Meir? I felt that his request humiliated me in front of my schoolmates, and I could not cope with it at all. The next morning I pretended to be ill, to the point where I actually managed to vomit. My mother let me stay home without really knowing what had happened, and so saved me from a responsibility which seemed to me beyond my capabilities as a small girl of tender age. Even today, when I recall the incident, I feel the same pain I did then, and I ask myself: What kind of morality is this, to cause a child to seethe with resentment, while you, the teacher, are unable to understand the emotional pressure you put on children when you expect them to shoulder responsibilities they are too young to bear or comprehend? The resentment I felt as a child continued to eat away at me, even in my early years in the United States.

During the first week of my life in America my husband and I went on a trip to Hollywood, which, to us, seemed not to be an earthly location at all but somewhere on another planet, which we could not imagine ever visiting. In the course of our trip we went into a shoe shop and I began to try on shoes. My husband looked at the shop assistant's Middle Eastern features and asked him where he was from.

"I'm an Israeli Jew," he replied.

I did not wait to consider what he had said. I dropped the shoe I was holding and ran one-shoed out of the shop as if wild animals were after me.

My husband caught up with me with my other shoe, shouting: "What's wrong, you idiot?"

I replied, trembling: "He's a Jew, and you want me to stay in his store?"

About two years after my flight to the United States, when my anger had not yet left me, my son's teacher called me two days before Christmas to tell me, "Wafa, although I'm Jewish by choice I give each of my pupils a small Christmas gift. I know you're Muslims and I don't want to upset you in any way— would you have any objection to my giving your son a present, too?"

At the time I had no idea what she meant by "Jewish by choice," as I could not imagine that people could choose their religion, but as soon as I heard her say "I'm Jewish" I was dumbfounded and quite unable to respond.

I kept saying to myself: My son's teacher is Jewish? What bad luck! I began to observe her closely so that if she did the slightest thing that displeased me I could report her to the school board and accuse her of discrimination. But Ms. Sparks, my son's teacher during his second year in the United States, was unable to demonstrate to me that she was anything other than an angel sent down from heaven to help my hearing-impaired son as a special-needs teacher.

Although I had a large number of similar experiences, I refused to allow any of them to change the attitudes I had acquired in thirty-two years in the land of my birth, which had led me to believe that Jews were criminals who cared only for killing and stealing money. One day my husband came home from work complaining of his bad luck. He had sold his car to a client who had given him a check for five hundred dollars. Only after he had accepted the check had he discovered that this client was Jewish, and now he told me he thought that the check would probably bounce. But this was not the end of the story, as I discovered the next day that I had washed my husband's shirt with the check in the pocket by mistake, and that nothing remained of the money except a few scraps of paper. My husband called the purchaser the following day and told him what had happened. Within less than half an hour he arrived at my husband's place of work and gave him five hundred dollars in cash, saying jokingly, "Man! Don't trust your wife! Next time I won't be able to replace the money."

We imbibed with our mothers' milk hatred for the Jews and for anyone who supported their cause. We justified this hatred by devising a conspiracy theory, and we called anyone who disagreed with us a Zionist agent. This conspiracy theory helped keep Muslims inside the straitjacket in which Islam had imprisoned their minds.

They did not hesitate to accuse anyone who tried to suggest new ideas or ways out of an existing stalemate of being an agent of international Zionism, and fears of this accusation prevented millions of Muslims from reexamining what they had been taught. I exchanged a number of e-mails with a reader of mine, a Muslim judge who lived in Iraq and admired my writing very much. As he had always seemed to me a broadminded and cultured man and had encouraged me a number of times to continue to write on Islamic issues, I was surprised when on one occasion he warned me against touching upon the Israeli-Palestinian conflict, lest I be accused of conspiring with Jews and Zionists. I wrote back thanking him for his advice, though declining to take it, and explained to him that I was utterly convinced that the reasons for the conflict were religious, and stemmed from the Prophet Muhammad's hostility toward the Jews.

In one of my messages to him I reminded him of the Koranic verse that reads: "The Jews say: 'Allah's hand is chained.'

May their own hands be chained! May they be cursed for what they say. By no means. His hands are both outstretched" (5:64).

I asked him, "Is that reasonable? What do you tell your son when you read that verse to him? How can you convince him that our problem with the Jews is their occupation of Palestine rather than Islam's attitude to them fourteen centuries before that occupation began?" The judge appeared to agree and understand to a great extent, though he still insisted that he was afraid I would be accused of conspiracy with Zionism and American imperialism if I expressed an opinion on the issue.

Islam's general attitude toward the Jews helped Muslims construct their conspiracy theory and use it as a weapon against anyone who tried to cast doubts upon the credibility and morality of Islamic teachings. With the aid of this weapon, they have been largely successful in attaining their objective.

II.

Every Muslim Must Be Carefully Taught

PEOPLE WHO LIVED in the environment that gave birth to Islam were paralyzed by their fears, which made every approaching moment seem like the prelude to a crushing war. People slept and woke in a state of expectation, fearing that their tribe was about to raid another. Their imagination could conceive of themselves only as killing or being killed. When Islam came along, it inflamed their fears, as it portrayed everyone whose origins were different from their own as a threat to their safety and stability, and as waiting only for an opportunity to do them harm. Their relationships with others were founded upon suspicion and doubt. Any relationship founded upon mistrust is bound to end in conflict. People living in a state of uncertainty interpret every stimulus in their environment on the basis of their suspicions, and regard everything that happens as proof that these suspicions are justified.

Paganism, Judaism, and Christianity were the religions of the inhabitants of the pre-Muslim Arabian Peninsula. When Muhammad appeared with his message, he threatened all those who did not follow him. He divided people into two groups. The first group was made up of those who believed in Allah and His Prophet and who would live in safety and peace in what was known as the "House of Peace" or paradise. The second group was made up of those who did not believe and who would live in a state of perpetual conflict in the House of War or enemy non-Muslim territory.

He vented his anger upon the followers of paganism, Judaism, and Christianity. His attitude toward these three varied in accordance with the strength of their adherents. From the start he left the pagans no option but death if they persisted in their religious observance. He said that they were weak and could be disregarded. Judaism and Christianity were better supported, stronger, and better organized, and so it was in his interests to adopt a more conciliatory attitude toward them. At first he adopted a moderate attitude toward them and acknowledged their religions as divinely inspired. The severity of his attitude to them varied with shifts in the balance of power between their followers and his own.

If you read the history and teachings of Islam you will get the initial impression that Islam is more accepting of and less hostile to Christians and Jews, as it recognizes the sanctity of their holy books. But anyone who scrutinizes this history carefully with a critical eye will realize that Islam has declared war on both religions, and has entrusted its followers with a sacred mission: to fight them until the End of Days.

Islamic teachings make no mention of Hinduism, Buddhism, or Zoroastrianism, even though these religions existed at the time and people practiced them. Muhammad, however, might never have heard of them. The more likely explanation is that they presented no threat to himself or his followers and, therefore, he displayed no aggression toward them.

As Islam acknowledged Judaism and Christianity, it might be supposed that it was more accepting of them and had more in common with them than it did with those who professed other religions. But the very opposite is the case. From the dawn of Islam until the present day, nothing has changed. Islam, naturally, is still hostile to all non-Muslims, but its enmity toward Jews and Christians is especially great. In order to maintain this state of enmity, Islam has fostered suspicion and mistrust among Muslims with regard to both Jews and Christians, by means of the Koranic verse that says: "You will please neither the Jews nor the Christians unless you follow their faith. Say: 'The guidance of Allah is the only guidance.' And if after all the knowledge you have been given you yield to their desires, there shall be none to help or protect you from the wrath of Allah" (2:120).

Jews and Christians, according to Islam, believe in the same God as Muslims do, but this does not work in their favor. Islam defines its relationship with them by their attitude to Muhammad, not by their attitude toward God. No Muslim, on the basis of the verse quoted above, can have a trusting relationship with a Jew or a Christian. The Koranic verse does not include any mention of other religions, and so the conflict remains at its most extreme with Jews and Christians, who in Muhammad's time refused to accept him as a prophet.

This verse played a decisive role in defining Muslim attitudes toward Jews and Christians and in coloring these attitudes with suspicion and doubt. It assured Muslims that Jews and Christians would never accept Muhammad, and so allows them no future opportunities to solve any conflict with the adherents of these two religions. When I was a young schoolchild, my religious education teacher urged us never to trust Jews or Christians. Their intentions, he assured us, were evil, as they never had accepted our prophet, and would never do so. Thus, from a young age, we were taught to be suspicious.

It is difficult, if not impossible, to have a healthy relationship with another person if you are suspicious of his or her intentions. No Muslim, no matter how well educated, no matter how outwardly accepting of others he may be, can free himself completely of his suspicions when circumstances bring him into contact with members of these two religions. He is quite convinced that he cannot have a real friendship with anyone who does not accept Muhammad as a divinely inspired prophet.

What was written about the Christians and especially the Jews constitutes the greater part of the Islamic heritage, the part that has held us back in a state of paranoia and hatred. From the dawn of Islam until the present day, mistrust of Jews and Christians has reduced Muslims to a state of paranoia that has reached a peak in the last fifty years, since the State of Israel was founded. With time the Jews have become a peg on which we hang our problems and our political, economic, military, and even moral misfortunes. Arab rulers, backed up by the clergy, have been the beneficiaries of this conspiracy theory, and every one of them has accused anyone who disagrees with him of treachery and conspiracy with the Zionist lobby. Members of the educated class, thinkers and writers—none of them are immune to this conspiracy theory: Whenever a writer comes up with an idea that does not conform to prevailing opinion, the rumor mill accuses him of being a Zionist agent.

The Syrian poet Nizar Kabbani wrote in one of his poems,

"Palestine was a broody hen for you, of whose precious eggs you ate . . ." Muslim men in general benefited from the conspiracy theory, which provided them with a justifiable reason for their failures in all areas of life, and relieved them of responsibility for them. Every Muslim man who gets a government job takes personal advantage such as a bribe, stealing money, abusing his authority or power on the grounds that he is busy preparing for the great battle against the "Zionist enemy."

At the hospital where I worked, the management decided to allocate a downstairs room as a daycare center for the children of the women who were doctors and nurses. One day all the children came down with infectious diarrhea and vomiting. The infection was caused by the unsanitary methods used to prepare water for the milk and to wash the feeding bottles. That same day we had a meeting with the administration manager. He had originally been a telephone operator at the hospital and had been promoted to a management position overnight. The secret of his promotion lay in the fact that his brother held a high post in the Syrian army. In the course of the meeting I brought up the issue of the contaminated water used to prepare the children's milk and the unsanitary methods used for washing the bottles, and suggested that we buy an electric sterilizer of a kind found in all the shops, which could hold twenty bottles at once.

I had hardly finished outlining my proposal when the manager leapt up like a wild animal that had been shot and began to rage and scream in my face: "Doctor, you appear to be unaware of the economic situation the country is in as a result of the unjust action taken against it by the international American and Zionist imperialists. Because of the positions held by our rightly guided government, they have imposed an international boycott on us, and we have to resist it by standing firm, supporting one another and trying to reduce government spending. You're suggesting we should buy an electric sterilizer? Heavens, how spoiled this generation is! Our mothers and grandmothers, may God have mercy on their souls, used to collect rainwater for us to drink. And look, we're like lions. Infections don't kill us, nor do illnesses!" As I came out of the meeting I thought to myself: Our mothers and grandmothers rode on donkeys and mules, but you, your lordship, drive around in a Mercedes and a BMW.

Doubt as to the sincerity of the good intentions of Americans in general and Jews in particular was one of the greatest obstacles I faced as I tried to adapt to my new surroundings as an immigrant in the United States. I spent my first few years in America in a fog of suspicion, unable to trust the people I was living among. I was utterly convinced that they were waiting for an opportunity to harm me, because I was a Muslim.

Shortly after my arrival, my American next door neighbor came and introduced himself to me, and learned my name and that of the town I came from. When I heard that he was a policeman I almost fainted, as I was convinced that once he realized I was a Muslim—he had not asked my religion—he would start to spy on me and make my life hell. And he really did make my life hell!

I began to watch him and his family, as a precaution against the unexpected. Every time a member of his family went into the front garden I would fear that my family and I were being spied upon, and I would watch through the peephole in the door or from behind the curtains. I was so tortured by suspicion that I decided we should look for another home. Then one morning I was surprised by my neighbor's knocking at my door.

"Good morning neighbor. I was wondering if you could possibly help me with something."

"What is it?"

"My gardener's Mexican and doesn't speak English, and I can't speak Spanish. Could you possibly translate what I want to ask him to do?"

"But I can't speak Spanish!"

He replied in amazement, "Don't you speak Spanish? Aren't you from South America?"

"No, I'm from Syria."

"Syria! Don't you speak Spanish in Syria?"

"No. We speak Arabic."

"I'm sorry, I had no idea."

Ninety percent of Americans do not think much about where Syria is on the map of the world, while 90 percent of Arabs believe that Americans spend most of their time spying on them and plotting to destroy Islam, so as to seize control of their oil and their resources.

In 1984 my husband and a group of his fellow lecturers were sent to England by the Syrian ministry of higher education to spend three months studying teaching methods at one of the universities there. While he was there, the British university lecturer responsible for the delegation invited the Syrians to lunch at his home, and proved himself a gracious host. A few months after my husband's return, this British lecturer visited

Syria and stopped over at the university where my husband taught. To show our appreciation of his earlier hospitality, my husband and I invited him to lunch at a restaurant near our home, at a cost equivalent to my husband's monthly salary. The lecturer's visit happened to coincide with our son's third birthday, and we had to put off buying the cake and the present until the following month.

But the financial pressures were not the only problem this visit caused us: The questions the university chancellor asked my husband about the invitation were even more stressful. The most distressing of them was: Did you consider, before you issued the invitation, that this man might be a British spy in the pay of international Zionism, and be planning to steal the university's scientific secrets or—who knows—perhaps military secrets, too? My husband and I experienced a period of anxiety that brought us to the verge of mental breakdown. Accusations of being Zionist agents—even if these were no more than rumors—could most certainly have destroyed our reputation and our future, if not our lives.

When I remember my childhood and reflect at length on our teachers' and clergymen's accusations against Jews in particular and Christians and other non-Muslims in general, I say to myself: If learned Muslims could replace the enormous quantities of hate contained in our schoolbooks, both religious and secular, with studies that focus on loving other people regardless of their religion, racial origin, or nationality, they would help to save the entire Muslim world from its backwardness, hunger, poverty, and ignorance. That hatred could well destroy us before it destroys our "enemies." For hatred is like acid in that it burns the container that holds it more than it damages the surface it is spilled upon.

When I criticize this style of education, most Muslims accuse me of being in the pay of the Jews and of receiving enormous sums to defend them. Of course, this accusation does not worry me in the least, as it is above all evidence of their inability to confront me with logical arguments. I am not defending the Jews so much as protecting the Muslims themselves. Why must children all over the Arab world drink in this hatred and waste the best years of their lives on thoughts of murder and revenge?

My three children received their primary education in American schools. None of them ever came home and told me their teachers had taught them that Muslims were terrorists and should be fought against. None of them learned that Christianity was the only true religion and that anyone who did not profess it was a heretic and an enemy. None of them learned in school that God hates Muslims.

I always ask myself: Why have my children, the product of American education, grown up to respect others, no matter what their religion, race, or origins? Why was I burned by the fires of hatred until late in life, and why are people in my homeland still being burned by that fire? Why should people in the land of my birth not learn to love, so that they can be productive, efficient, and happy like people in other countries that teach love? Why should people in my homeland not learn to accept people who do not profess the same religion as they do, so that they can live with others in peace and harmony? We have learned to hate others, and this hatred has hurt us more than it has hurt anyone else.

When I was in fourth grade in primary school, Syria received aid from the UN food aid agency that included trucks of Nestlé's powdered milk manufactured in the United States. One of the conditions attached to this aid would appear to have been that the milk had to be distributed free to primary schoolchildren since, if this condition was not attached, Syrian officials would sell the trucks of milk and pocket the money as usual. The milk began to be distributed to us schoolchildren at an average rate of one glass per pupil per day, which we had to drink before the end of that school day. I remember our teacher telling us at every lesson, "Can you imagine what's happening here? America donates milk to Syrian children to fool the world into believing it's generous, but to Israeli children it donates tanks!" Most of us did not drink the milk; instead we poured it out on the unpaved earth of the playground.

Today I can find no explanation for our refusal to drink the American milk other than a psychological repugnance for the United States and its milk as a result of the venom that our teachers had poured into our tender minds. Why do we inject our children with this poison? That is the question that has confronted me ever since I began to discover the truth in my new society. When I scream at the top of my voice, "Stop injecting this poison!" I am doing so not just to protect Jews and Christians. I am doing it above all to protect the children of my homeland and save them from being burned by the acid of hatred that scorched my generation.

I can still clearly remember our religious education teacher's repeating to us sayings and stories of the Prophet Muhammad that deal with Jews and Christians, and I can recall the effect these anecdotes had on our consciences and mental well-being. The story most deeply etched in my memory is the one that relates how Muhammad and a group of his followers heard a far-off sound. The prophet's followers asked him: "What's that noise, Oh Prophet of God?" and he replied: "That's the Jews suffering torment in their graves" (Sahih Bukhari, 1286).

In another hadith Muhammad says: "An imposter will come along and claim to be the messiah, and seventy thousand Jews will follow him, each girt with a sword. But then the messiah will catch him, kill him, and defeat all the Jews. Each and every stone and tree will say: 'Oh servant of Allah, Oh Muslim, here is a Jew, come and kill him.'" The only exception is the salt tree, which is one of the trees of the Jews, and if they hide behind it, it will not reveal their presence. Today there are Muslims who like to spread the rumor that Jews in Israel know the truth of this hadith and have begun to plant salt trees to hide behind.

Whenever Muhammad wanted to stop his followers from doing something, he would say: "God has cursed the Jews because they did that." He said, for example: "God cursed the Jews because they took the graves of their prophets as a place for prayer" (Sahih Muslim, 823). A man asked one day: "Oh Prophet of God, I have a slave girl whom I desire and to whom I wish to do what a man does, but, for fear she may become pregnant, I ejaculate outside her body. But I have heard that ejaculating outside a woman is considered tantamount to murder of the fetus—is that true?"

He replied in a hadith: "May God curse the Jews, as they said that! Pay no attention to them, and ejaculate where you will. If God wished her to become pregnant you would not be able to ejaculate outside her body." If education is responsible for shaping the human mind, then the entire mind is the product of education. What sort of mind can teachings such as these produce?

Is not the Muslim the natural product of his education?

12.

Clash of Civilizations

THE SEPTEMBER 11TH terrorist attacks shocked me, but they did not surprise me. Day and night, I had been expecting something of the kind. I had been expecting it because of my involvement with what was being written in the Arabic-language newspapers here and what was being said at our social get-togethers. In the Arab world, there is no such thing as a secret, and everything that is about to happen in the future is preceded by signs and portents in the present. But many people cannot read the signs, for one of two reasons: either conceit or ignorance. American government officials prior to September 11th were conceited and ignorant enough to disregard them.

A traditional Arab folktale tells the story of a man who was riding through the desert when another traveler, who had lost his way, signaled to him to stop and pick him up. Experience had taught the desert Arabs to beware of highwaymen. Nonetheless, the horseman took pity on the wayfarer and stopped to pick him up. After a short time had passed the wayfarer said to the horseman, "What a fine horse you have, my friend." A little later the wayfarer said again, "This is indeed a fine horse, my friend." After an additional period of time had elapsed, the wayfarer said, "By God, this really is a fine horse we have here!"

The horseman pulled up at once and told the wayfarer, "Get off my horse or I'll kill you! At first you said what a fine horse 'you have,' then you called it 'this horse,' and now you said what a fine horse 'we have.' In another minute you'll be calling it 'my horse,' and kicking me off its back!" Americans do not have enough experience of highway robbers and so they allow any passing wayfarer to violate the sanctity of their horses! They are not expert at either debate or trickery. They say what they mean and they mean what they say, and have no idea that they are dealing with people skilled in saying what they don't mean and meaning what they have never said.

Laws alone cannot safeguard a society. For a law to be effective, there must be a moral foundation in the populace, and a nation has to attain a certain moral standard before it can either make laws or apply them. It is a society's morals that formulate its laws and guarantee their enforcement. Interpersonal relationships within a society are complex, and the laws that govern that society may not be able to deal with every individual case. Only morality can do that. When I moved from a still primitive society to a civilized one I was impressed by the enormous difference between the two. It was then I began to search, as I still do today, for the reasons behind these differences.

I emerged from my search utterly convinced that what we are experiencing in Muslim societies is not a crisis of government, revenue, resources, or even law: It is a moral crisis. Our Muslim societies are governed by a religious law that imposes itself by force and relies on fear as a means of perpetuating and protecting itself. Islam, as I have already emphasized, was born in an arid and desolate environment where people had to struggle to survive. It adopted the customs of that environment and that era, absorbed them, and then refused to allow them to change with the times.

Culture encompasses religion and adapts it to suit the times. American culture was influenced by Christianity and Judaism—and, indeed, it still is—but it changes nonetheless in accordance with the times, and religion changes with it. It is culture that shapes religion, not the other way around. As soon as religion begins to interfere in people's lives and take them over, it loses its spirituality and reveals its inability to keep up with people's constantly changing needs. Muslim clergymen confront us on the television screen and talk about Islam's attitudes to menstruation, the advantages of banks, the Pakistani nuclear bomb, and tsunamis, all in the same breath.

Islam subjugated the cultures of all the peoples it afflicted, but it eradicated all traces of indigenous Arab culture more thoroughly than those of any other. This culture no longer possesses any of its original distinguishing features; over the course of fourteen centuries, it is Muslim law that has delineated its characteristics. A Christian born and brought up in Jordan is more Islamic in his behavior and way of thinking than a Pakistani Muslim. Islam, as I said before, damaged the cultures of all the Muslim peoples, but, since the Koran was written in Arabic and its translation into any other language is forbidden, Islam was unable totally to blot out the characteristics of other cultures in quite the same way it erased Arab culture.

Non-Arab Muslim peoples have managed to preserve the remnants of their cultures and protect them from Islamization.

These remnants, sparse and meager though they may be, distinguished these nations from the Arab peoples, who, as they were more profoundly influenced by Islam, were much more seriously damaged. This was the situation from the inception of Islam until thirty years ago, i.e., until the Saudi Wahhabi octopus, with its terrorist ideology and its funding, infiltrated these nations and the non-Arab Muslim nations of their cultures, such as Indonesia.

Islam is a legal code that was created in an era when a mentality of raiding and booty held sway, and, as a result, its pivotal issues are raiding and spoils. It was unable to construct any common foundation of morality; rather, it dealt a death blow to all the finer moral qualities of the pre-Islamic Arabs.

Antara al-Absi, one of the most famous of the pre-Islamic Arab poets, boasted in a self-glorifying poem in which he enumerates his own virtues, that he considered the most important of these to be his "abstinence from spoils." His era was followed by the Islamic period, which adopted a culture that canonized raiding and incursions and put its prophet Muhammad and God in the same category as far as division of the spoils was concerned, allocating them a one fifth share between them.

Whatever strictures it might contain, this legal code could not escape the limitations of this mentality. Men killed others so as not to be killed themselves, and robbed so as not to die of starvation. Muhammad was a warrior rather than a thinker. He left no moral legacy for his followers to build upon or use as a basis for the societies they founded. Nor did he leave them room outside the boundaries of this law in which they might have exercised their freedom and perhaps, responding to the demands of time, have invented a moral code of their own.

The most important traditions written and handed down about Muhammad concern his raids and what happened in the course of them. All his teachings stem from the realities of the world he lived in and are the indisputable product of it.

If you read the biography of the Prophet from beginning to end you will find no trace of any kind of moral authority. Some people may protest that it has to be read in its historical context. But morals, by definition, do not change with the changing times. Unlike culture, they are not subject to the dictates of time or place, but remain applicable everywhere, at any time. Morals are a common code shared by all peoples of the world at all times in all places. What is moral in Beverly Hills will be considered moral in the tribes of Africa, and vice versa. Culture may vary from nation to nation and country to country, but the moral code is almost identical everywhere at all times.

The moral code is a set of natural laws that enjoin people to do what is right and avoid what is wrong. When nature drew them up, it equipped people with a rational or instinctive ability to distinguish between right and wrong, so that they could adhere to these laws. Following this code helps the human species to survive in safety.

Fear, of all the emotions, is one of the most destructive to the human spirit. When people fall victim to fear they lose their ability to tell right from wrong, as their every action is reduced to a reaction to their fear. In the desert environment that gave birth to Islam, human thought and behavior reflected the fears characteristic of life in those surroundings. The fact that people did not feel safe gave rise to all the customs that dominated that time and place, as a reaction to this destructive emotion.

The great catastrophe came with the advent of Islam, which gave these customs divine sanction and laid a sharp divisive sword between those who accepted them and those who did not. Anyone who openly rejected any one of these Islamic customs was considered an apostate and was punished by death. Islam resorted to the use of fear as a means of controlling its adherents and added to their existing fear of their arid desert environment the fear of the sword, and it was this that deprived Muslims of the ability to tell right from wrong.

A society in which people lose their ability—rational or instinctive—to distinguish between right and wrong becomes a curse to all humanity. All religions undermined Man's ability to tell right from wrong when they taught him to fear God's punishment should he consider rejecting any of their teachings.

Islam, however, differs from other religions in that it threatens its followers not just with hell but also with death, in order to speed their journey to hell. People are more frightened of death than they are by the idea of being punished by God. Muslims followed Muhammad's teachings blindly, for fear of feeling the sword at their throat. Muhammad told his followers in a hadith: "Drink camel urine, it contains the cure for all ills." Muslims can graduate from the most famous medical schools in the world yet still believe that camel urine can cure illness. Their belief does not stem in most cases from scientific conviction but from fear of the deadly sword.

In fourteen hundred years no Muslim has dared candidly to exercise his ability to distinguish right from wrong and tell his fellow believers: "Don't drink camel urine!" Primary-school teachers read their pupils the account which relates: "The

Prophet Muhammad married the Jewish woman Safia on the day her husband, father and brother were killed," without engaging in any discussion of the morality or legitimacy of such a marriage. Muslims believe, as an article of faith, that everything that the Prophet Muhammad said and did was inspired by God. Islam does not permit any one of its followers to doubt that these words and deeds are right by the moral standards of all times and places.

Let me relate a story from Ibn al Athir, an Arab Muslim historian, on the life of Muhammad: "Muhammad, God bless him and grant him salvation, sent five of his men to kill Kaab Bin al-Ashraf who had been lampooning him and inciting the tribe of Quraysh against him. One of the five was Kaab's brother Abu Naila. Muhammad accompanied them to a place named Baqi' al-Gharqad then sent them off, saying, 'Go in the name of God. May God aid them' and then returned home.

"When the five men reached Kaab's camp, Abu Naila called out to him and Kaab jumped up in his blanket and came out, feeling safe because he had heard his brother's voice. But the men betrayed him and killed him. They took his head and made their way back to Baqi' al-Gharqad (that is, the place where Muhammad had left them), and said 'God is great.' Muhammad, God bless him and grant him salvation, heard them and said, 'God is great,' for he knew that they had killed Kaab. When they reached Muhammad, God bless him and grant him salvation, he was at prayer. He told them, 'You have succeeded honorably,' and they flung Kaab's head into his hands."

When a Muslim reads this story, no matter how well educated and informed he may be, he finds nothing in it that makes him curious enough to ask: "Where in this story is the mission with which God entrusted his prophet?" When terrorists in Iraq and other Muslim countries behead their hostages without any apparent qualms, the world asks: "Why do they do it?" Muslims who describe themselves as moderates reply: "These terrorists have misunderstood the teachings of Islam." But I ask: Have they misunderstood the story of how Muhammad's companions killed Kaab Bin al-Ashraf, then tumbled his head into Muhammad's hands?

If Zarqawi has misunderstood what Muhammad has said, as some Muslims claim, has he also misunderstood what he did? Hundreds of stories like the account of Kaab's murder fill biographies of the prophet, which serve as the main—if not the only—source of learning in the Muslim world. Umm Qirfa was a woman who, most Muslim historians agree, was over a hundred years old when Muhammad's followers, at his request, because she had written a poem against him, tied her legs to two camels and drove them in opposite directions until she was torn limb from limb. Muslims take pride in this murder, which they regard as an indication of Muhammad's followers' loyalty to Islam. This cultural fund of Muhammad's words and deeds has remained for fourteen centuries the "moral compass" of every Muslim, wherever he may be.

An Arab proverb says: You can extricate a man who has sunk into a quagmire, but it is impossible to remove a quagmire that has sunk into a man. People in the Islamic world have absorbed the quagmire in its entirety and are experiencing a moral crisis. They badly need to be able to feel guilt for the sins they commit. Some people may ask: What has Islam to do with this crisis? Islam remains what it has always been: the main, if not the only, source of education in the Muslim world, and people are the product of their education.

When I delve into the Muslim books that were the main source from which we quenched our thirst for cultural knowledge, I begin to doubt the efficacy of the methods America and the rest of the world are using to combat terrorism. The Americans went to Iraq to search for weapons of mass destruction, and announced that they had found none. They found none not because they did not exist, but because the searchers did not know where they were hidden. Had they opened any Muslim book they would have found in it vast quantities of such weapons.

The danger lies not in the weapons themselves, but in the hand that grasps them. American troops cannot remove this threat that faces all humankind unless the world remains alert and is aware of where in the Islamic world the weapons of mass destruction lie concealed. The schools responsible for creating the terrorist mentality in the Muslim world are more dangerous than any weapons factory on earth. These schools have destroyed people's minds, and this destruction has a greater effect on their own lives than its does on the lives of others. The terrorist mentality is a barren one, which can produce nothing of any worth, and so it has a greater effect on the lives of those who adopt it than it does on the lives of their enemies.

No Westerner can fully comprehend the truth of what I have said here, because Westerners do not live in the Muslim world and so find it hard to imagine the extent of the moral disintegration afflicting all aspects of life in these societies. People in these societies have lost their ability to feel guilt for their misdeeds. From their earliest youth they have been brainwashed by teachings that have convinced them that God has created them to be slaves.

As long as he prays, fasts, and reads the Koran, a Muslim feels that he has done his duty, as his sense of responsibility does not extend beyond the performance of these specified commandments. The rulers of all Muslim countries lie to their subjects and plunder, murder, and torture them. But on Fridays and religious holidays they never fail to go to the mosque and pray. No Muslim clergyman will utter a word of criticism of the behavior of these leaders—unless, of course, the leader happens to belong to a different religious denomination. Saddam Hussein murdered hundreds of thousands of Kurds and Shiites, but the only Muslims we have heard protesting against his crimes have been Shiites.

Anyone who browses through the pages of Muslim history from the day Muhammad first declared his new religion until the present day will see at once how bloody it has been. Muslims themselves have spilled more of one another's blood than anyone else. As young schoolchildren we would recount the stories of fighting and killing we had learned from our history books and books of Muslim teachings with the same enthusiasm that we played hide and seek. We took as much delight in repeating the phrase "then he drew his sword and cut off his head" as an American child does in a bar of chocolate, but we experienced no sense of fear as we did so, nor did we question the legitimacy of all that killing.

We became familiar with the language of murder and terrorism and grew addicted to it. We were as proficient in it as a surgeon is at opening a patient's chest to remove a growth. An ordinary person does not split open another's person chest unless he is either a criminal totally lacking in human conscience or a surgeon whose medical knowledge and scientific expertise guide him as he carries out his humane mission. We no longer condemn the language of killing and terrorism, which has become a way of life for us. It has become a skill that we practice with the same delight that the surgeon takes in his work.

Just imagine an American child standing in class and saying to his teacher: "I'll cut my enemy's head off with this sword." How would the teacher and the other pupils react? All aspects of life in our Islamic culture are a reflection of this philosophy of death. In 2005 I paid a visit to Syria. In Damascus, while I was sitting in the bus waiting to leave for a neighboring town, I watched a small boy of no more than eight get on carrying a bundle of newspapers to sell to the passengers. "Forty American soldiers reported killed in a heroic suicide bombing in Baghdad!" he shouted, in an attempt to arouse their interest. I quickly took a paper and scanned it keenly while the boy jumped off the bus and vanished into the crowd.

I went through the paper from beginning to end but found no mention of the death of any American soldiers. In the midst of my astonishment I overheard another passenger say, "The little bastard duped us!" Even a boy as young as eight fully understands the psychology of his people and knows precisely how to play upon their emotions. The death of forty American soldiers in Baghdad is hot news that Syrians will pay the price of a loaf of bread to read about in the paper.

The average Syrian today cares about nothing beyond making a living. He exists in a state of appalling mental lethargy, is uninvolved in world events, and appears to be unconcerned by them. Nonetheless, the death of forty American soldiers is a hot topic that can penetrate even his apathy. Children in Syria are an important source of family income. From a very early age they are aware of market forces and fully understand which issues kindle the interest of their fellow countrymen. It is very sad that even children as young as eight are so profoundly affected by the prevailing mental disintegration that they make up news in order to sell papers! Men in the Arab world lack responsibility for the moral growth of their children.

A high-ranking officer in the Syrian army ran over my six-year-old niece as he drove his car at an insane speed through a busy part of town. Once, by chance, I heard him speak about the accident. He laid the blame on the little girl, who, he said, had crossed the road on her way to school without checking to ensure that the way was clear. He also tried to discredit the family by claiming that her parents had been negligent and had failed to teach her how to cross the road properly.

I can still remember the lack of respect with which some members of our emergency room medical staff used to treat the crushed bodies of road-accident victims. I recall how, on one occasion that I shall never forget as long as I live, a ten-year-old girl was brought into the emergency room where I worked as a doctor. She was a servant in a private home, and her master had sent her out to buy a pack of cigarettes from the nearby shop. As she crossed the road a garbage truck ran her down and cut off one of her legs. The little girl died on the operating table, and her family took possession of her body. A couple of hours later, as I was throwing away some soiled bandages, I was horrorstruck to see the girl's leg in the trash can. Investigation revealed that the orderly responsible for taking patients to the operating theater had, without any pangs of conscience, thrown the leg away as, he said, there was no point taking it into the operating theater with her as the doctors could not reattach it.

Never in my life have I heard or read of a Muslim man's expressing feelings of guilt about something he has done, even in fiction. People feel guilt only when they feel a sense of responsibility and acknowledge that they have made a mistake. But Muslims are infallible: The mere fact that they are Muslim makes their every error pardonable. A man's adherence to Islam is defined not by his actions and responsibilities, but only by the profession of faith he recites: "I testify that there is no god but God, and that Muhammad is the messenger of God." As long as he continues to repeat this profession of faith he will continue to be a Muslim, and no crime he may commit against others can diminish this. Saddam Hussein was one of the great tyrants of history, but most Sunni Muslims consider him a martyr. At his funeral they chanted: "To paradise, oh beloved of God."

The first moral lesson a person learns is the difference between the concepts "yes" and "no"—in other words, the ability to decide what to accept and what to reject. Human beings learn this lesson in the first year of their lives, and it is considered to be the foundation that will subsequently support the entire structure of their morality. The solidity of this foundation is what determines the soundness of the entire edifice and its ability to withstand life's challenges.

A Muslim lives his whole life and dies without ever having learned this lesson. Islamic culture has no clear concept of "yes" and "no." The two opposites are confused in a way that makes

Muslims' behavior incomprehensible to others who interact with them. Muslim culture replaces these two concepts with a third, which combines and mixes the two and blurs the distinction between them as mutually exclusive opposites. This third concept is expressed by the formula *inshallah* (God willing). If you ask a Muslim a question that requires the answer yes or no, he will reply inshallah. Inshallah does not necessarily mean either yes or no. It means that the answer lies with God, and God will decide. The expression *inshallah* allows Muslims to avoid taking responsibility. They cannot be held responsible for any decision they may make, as God has made it for them, and its outcome, whether good or bad, is the will of God. If you ask a Muslim, "Would you like to join us for lunch tomorrow?" he will answer inshallah. Of course, he is not necessarily saying "Yes, I'll come" or "No, I won't come." If he does come to lunch, it will be because God has enabled him to come, and if he does not come, that, too, will be the result of divine predestination, and no one has any right to protest!

On my last visit to Syria, I was spending an evening with my brother's family when my nine-year-old niece Sarah surprised me with a barrage of questions about America in general and Hollywood in particular.

"Do you know Whitney Houston? Have you heard her latest song? I like Nicole Kidman, but her marriage to Tom Cruise hasn't worked out very well!"

"Which Britney Spears song do you like best?"

In the end I was asking the questions and she was supplying the answers, as she turned out to know Hollywood a great deal better than I know my own home or the dishes in my own kitchen.

I asked her, "Why don't you come and visit me in the United States so that you can go to Hollywood?"

She gasped and her eyes glowed like stars on a dark night. "Can I?"

"Of course," I said. "It would be my pleasure and I'll foot the bill for your trip."

Sarah ran to her mother and asked her, "Mommy, can I visit my aunt in America?" Then, without giving her mother time to reply, she continued, "And please don't say inshallah!"

Everyone burst out laughing, but, as for me, I wept! Sarah submitted an application for a visa to the American Embassy in Damascus, and was turned down. She called me, sobbing, and told me, "Auntie, I'm unhappy. God doesn't want me to come and see you in America!" This is the first time that God has been blamed for an offense committed by America, rather than the other way round!

My niece, despite her tender years at the time, was perfectly aware that inshallah meant neither yes nor no. She begged her mother not to use the expression, which, as far as she was concerned, expressed only a vagueness that her young mind could not accept. She would have preferred her mother to say no rather than inshallah.

A nod and a smile may or may not signify assent. When an Arab revokes his agreement he justifies himself by insisting that he had never agreed in the first place, as he had not said yes, but had merely smiled and nodded his head. This ambiguity means that Muslims' relationships with others are capricious and uncertain, and this has made it hard for people to trust them. People who cannot differentiate between yes and no and can express neither unambiguously have a confused notion of concepts in general. Their moral infrastructure becomes brittle and is liable to collapse under the pressure of any question that has to be answered by yes or no. This moral fragility afflicts Muslims today, and they find it hard to interact with the modern world, which constantly confronts them with questions that require them to accept or decline—to respond either "yes" or "no"—clearly and unambiguously.

The second time I was interviewed by Al Jazeera after I appeared on the show dealing with the clash of civilizations, the interviewer asked me, "Do you mean that this is a clash between the backwardness of the Muslims and modern civilization as exemplified by the West?" I answered without hesitation, "Yes, that's what I mean." This reply generated enough reactions from the Arab world to fill a book.

One of the most curious responses was an e-mail from an Egyptian lawyer, who wrote: "When I heard the question I didn't think for a moment you'd say anything but, 'No, that's not what I meant, you misunderstood me,' and then I expected you to beat about the bush, as Muslims don't go in for direct answers! But when I heard your reply I lost my mind and danced around the room like a madman shouting, 'What a disaster, what a disaster!'" You cannot ask a man in the Muslim world a question whose response requires the assumption of any kind of responsibility and expect to get an unequivocal "yes" or "no" in reply.

Many years ago, before I came to live in America, I heard a Western journalist ask President Hafez al-Assad in the course of an interview she was conducting with him, "If you reach a peace agreement with Israel, will your country establish diplomatic relations with it?" Assad began to equivocate and did not give a clear answer. The journalist asked him again, "Mr.

President, can you reply with a 'yes' or 'no'?" But he continued to beat about the bush until finally, with a certain display of irritation, she gave up and moved on to the next question. When people cannot clearly distinguish between "yes" or "no," they lose their credibility. As a result they cannot sustain healthy and successful relationships with other people. People are tied to their promises by their tongues, not their anklebones.

Relationships in Muslim societies are governed by interest and necessity, rather than by any sincerity on the part of the people conducting them. Such relationships are as ambiguous as the expression *inshallah*, which we've already discussed and which you will hear constantly wherever you go in the Muslim world. All aspects of life in these societies reflect the lack of sincerity that governs interpersonal relationships within them. When people fail to keep their promises they put the blame on God, saying it was not his will, and justify this by adding, "You misunderstood me. When I said inshallah I didn't mean I would do such-and-such."

On my most recent visit to Syria two years ago I realized the truth of the French proverb: "A fish cannot see the water it swims in." I swam in the Syrian sea for thirty-three years of my life, and was apparently unable to see the water I was swimming in. When I returned to it after fifteen years of living in America, however, I saw it clearly for what it was. Although, of course, it was my dissatisfaction with life there that made me want to emigrate, I did not at the time fully understand the nature and causes of my discontent. It was my experiences in the United States that allowed me, after fifteen years' absence, to see the true nature of the waters I once swam in.

I plunged deep into these waters and used my ability to put things under a microscope to analyze its constituents in detail. What I saw was not very different from a colony of bacteria such as we used to observe under a microscope in the microbiology lab when I was at medical school. Though people may disapprove of this comparison, it is apt nonetheless. A society that is not governed by the rule of law, but by the law of the jungle: the strong devour the weak, and both justify the status quo as inevitable divine decree.

I met up with a woman who had been a close friend before I left Syria. At the time, she, like me, was in unenviable financial circumstances. When we met once more I was surprised to find that she had attained a high position in the Syrian government and that gold and silver had rained down upon her ever since. Rumor had it that she had been appointed to the post because of a suspect relationship with an influential man, despite the fact that she was married and the mother of children.

I visited her at her home, where she made me very welcome. Never in my life had I seen such luxury as I saw there, and I was amazed at the magnificence of the building and its appointments. She began to tell me of her adventures in Europe and showed me the jewels she had bought on her travels. I had intended to bring up the subject of the tragic situation of the Syrian people, and asked her unhesitatingly, "Samira, is it right that you should live such a fabulous life while nine out of ten Syrians are suffering?" She answered with no sign of shame, "But that's God's destiny, Wafa. Only he knows why."

I asked, "What has God got to do with it?"

"Do you refuse to acknowledge God's will, Wafa? You must have become Americanized." Then she tried to change the subject by asking, "Which perfume do you like best? I've got lots of different kinds and I'd like to give you some of them."

I replied jokingly, "Yes, I have become Americanized, and in America, Samira, people don't wear perfume but eat and drink by the sweat of their brow!"

The Islamic nations suffered the consequences of this stagnation, as Muslims were reduced to programmed automatons unfit for either their time or place. This situation posed no problems for the rest of the world until the end of the twentieth century and the beginning of the twenty-first. At the start of the two final decades of the last century, the new technologies that facilitated travel and communications shrank the world, until, by the beginning of the present century, it had been reduced to the dimensions of a small village. As our global home contracted, Muslims found themselves in face-to-face encounters with outsiders to whom Islamic law and teachings were utterly foreign, and have shown themselves unable to adjust to this new reality.

About thirty years ago the Syrian authorities constructed a railroad network that linked the country's eastern provinces to Aleppo Province in the north. As it plied this route, the train traveled for vast distances through the Syrian Desert, which is inhabited by Bedouin herders and their livestock. As a result, a strange phenomenon occurred: These Bedouin took to stoning the train as it passed through their villages, breaking car windows and attacking the passengers. They would continue to pursue the train and pelt it with rocks until it had passed, when they would flee and vanish among their tents.

This state of affairs continued for years, and the Syrian

authorities were obliged to appoint inspectors and special forces to track down the Bedouin responsible. When I look back and recall that period, I can interpret the Bedouin's behavior only as motivated by a fear engendered by this strange mechanical monster's intrusion into their desert world, which had hitherto been shrouded in an unchanging silence. They regarded the roar of the train as an invasion of their privacy and a genuine threat to their way of life, and so tried to protect their world by destroying the train and breaking its windows, with total disregard for the safely of the passengers.

This is exactly what happened to Muslims living in their unchanging worlds. Overnight, nomads roaming the Empty Quarter (the Great Sandy Desert of the Arabian Peninsula) were catapulted from the backs of their camels to airplane seats, and found themselves in the streets of Paris, New York, or Copenhagen. Back home they woke up one morning and peeped out of their tents to discover outlandish heavy machinery drilling holes in their desert to search for oil, under the direction of people who resembled no one and nothing they had ever seen before. The sight terrified them, and they saw it as a threat to their belief system and way of life.

Muslims have been unable to adapt to the world in its new form, and have found themselves obliged, both at home in their own countries and as immigrants abroad, to adopt a new way of life incompatible with their religious laws and beliefs. Both acceptance and rejection of this new order entailed an appalling psychological struggle.

On the one hand, Western technology has provided Muslims in abundance with a lifestyle they had never dreamed of, and on which they have come to depend. But, on the other hand, this new way of life bears no relation and is not compatible whatsoever with the teachings, concepts, and religious laws they grew up with.

This struggle is most intensely exemplified in Muslims whose fate it is to live outside their homelands. In these people, this conflict has produced a form of depression and unhappiness that one notices immediately in all Muslims living in the West as soon as one gets to know them a little and begins to probe the depths of their psyche. This internal struggle has left these Muslims prey to questions for which they have no answers. They are torn between acceptance and rejection of life among people whom their beliefs do not allow them to trust or accept as friends or superiors at work: Islam categorically forbids Muslims to accept a job in a workplace where their boss will be a non-Muslim. Life in the West has improved the Muslim's standard of living and guaranteed his children a brighter future than their peers in the Muslim world can expect, but at the same time it has exposed these children to a way of life that Muslim religious law finds unacceptable.

This conflict leaves Muslims with a sense of frustration. Whenever I noticed signs of this frustration I would engage the concerned individual in a discussion of the American way of life and the differences between Muslim and Western society. My attempts were not intended to produce any result, which would have been beyond my abilities. Rather, they stimulated these people and drew them into conversation, in the course of which I could uncover the secrets that lay hidden in the depths of their psyche. With time this frustration would give way to a terrible anger against everything around them in their new society.

The editor of a Los Angeles Arabic-language newspaper once wrote in response to an article of mine: "America has dazzled her ... Life in a morally impoverished society has blinded her," and subsequently published a number of readers' opinions in the same vein, all of which described American society as morally weak and the women who belong to it as a saleable commodity, and concluded that "Wafa Sultan appears to admire these women." I had once met the wife of this editor, several years before he launched his attack on me. She told me that they had fled to the United States to escape the civil war in Lebanon after she had lost both her brother and sister in the conflict, and her husband, the editor, had lost several members of his family.

Of course, many people in the West may be unaware that the Lebanese civil war lasted for seventeen years, cutting down the young and devouring the elderly, and killing, maiming, and displacing over a million people in a country whose total population did not exceed 4 million. History has not witnessed a more squalid war than this one. Victims were selected on the basis of identity. Identity cards in Lebanon indicate not only a person's religion, but also the specific denomination or community to which they belong. Those who had no identity card in their pocket were killed on the basis of their name, for in Lebanon, as in most Muslim countries, a person's name indicates which religious community he or she belongs to.

The respected editor and his pregnant wife fled the country and sought refuge in America. His wife confessed that they had been living on welfare up until the time I met her. She told me alarming stories of how she and her family had been treated by members of the Arab diaspora here, and complained of the arguments these Arabs had brought with them from their countries of origin. Nonetheless, her husband spared no efforts in championing their morals, conventions, and traditions when he read my article defending my adoptive society, the opportunities it had allowed us, and the highly moral way with which it had welcomed and treated us. But this is always the Muslim attitude, which is encapsulated in the Arabic proverb: "Even though he sees it fly, he insists the duck is a goat," or, in other words: "None so blind as those who will not see."

However tightly they cling to life in their new society and no matter how comfortable and carefree their life under the protection of that society's laws may be, they will still insist that Westerners are immoral, while Muslims are bound by moral habits and customs. If you ask them, "Why, then, do Muslim women apply to American courts in cases of divorce and child custody?" they reply, "This particular woman is an anomaly. She's not representative of Muslim women as a whole."

Muslim women living in the United States do not usually tolerate ill treatment at the hands of their husbands. Instead of accepting it submissively as they would in their homelands, they seek a divorce settlement in an American court. They use the laws of their adoptive society to wrest custody of their children away from their husbands and force them to pay child support. But this very same woman, were you to ask for her opinion of the moral climate of her adoptive society, would subject you to endless lectures vilifying American morals and praising Islamic law and morality as exemplified in Muslim society.

I once stopped for an oil change at an auto repair shop in Long Beach, California. The owner was a young Palestinian, and most of his workers were Arabic-speaking youngsters. While I was waiting my turn a car pulled up and a young man of Middle Eastern aspect alighted and tossed out a greeting in Arabic, to which the garage owner replied indignantly, "Why are you late? We've been waiting for you since morning."

The young man replied, "I got my American citizenship this morning, and I've just got back from taking the oath of allegiance."

I looked at him and said in Arabic, "Congratulations!"

He gave me a contemptuous look and asked, "What are you congratulating me for? American citizenship is worth less than the sole of this shoe," and he pointed to his foot.

I could not disguise my annoyance, and told him, "But you've just pledged your allegiance to this country and chosen to take its citizenship of your own free will!"

He asked me in bewilderment, "Are you a Muslim, sister?"

"Is religion relevant to the issue?" I inquired. We went on arguing for over half an hour, until I found myself driving out of the garage like the wind, shaking with fury. About five months after this incident I heard that this man's son had committed suicide in mysterious circumstances, at the age of twenty. His body was found in a public park with the pistol he had used to shoot himself lying beside him. He had left a letter for his parents in his office drawer. Rumors spread through the Arabic-speaking community to the effect that his father had been behind his suicide. He had forced him to live an austere life in accordance with the teachings of Islamic law, and the young man had fallen into a state of depression six months before he died by his own hand.

Muslims differ from the adherents of all other religions in both the quality and degree of their loyalty to their religion. I have no doubt that some of them have already freed themselves from the bonds imposed by Islam and have begun to enjoy a freer and more open lifestyle either in their homelands or in the countries to which they have emigrated. But no matter how different their individual lifestyles may be, these Muslims are united in their degree of loyalty to their religion. If you strike up a conversation with the most open of them and point out that some of the teachings of Islam contradict the most basic things about the life they are now leading, they will not hesitate for a moment to express the conviction that they themselves are at fault. The error lies, they will say, not in Muslim teachings, but in their own behavior, which differs so greatly from what these teachings impose.

This internal conflict has exacted a high price from Muslims. Exposure to modern life has disorientated them psychologically and left them with a sense of regret. They feel this regret because they are pursuing a lifestyle that contradicts the teachings of their religion at the most fundamental level, on the one hand, and because they have not followed these teachings to the letter on the other. They do not want to admit that the modern lives they lead are much better than their life under the laws of Islam, nor do they want to acknowledge that the teachings of that law are not compatible with a productive and efficient modern lifestyle. They do not know which to choose and continue to bestride two horses galloping in opposite directions.

Before oil was discovered in the Gulf States, Muslims lived a primitive existence. Then, in the twinkling of an eye, the modern world descended upon their campsites, disfigured their world with its palaces, high-rises, cars, and technology, and threatened the unchanging silence of their environment. Dubai lies at the heart of the desert where Islam was born. What was Dubai about thirty years ago but an arid desert with no trace of life? And what is it today? Today it is one of the world's largest commercial centers. It costs seventy dollars just to walk into one of its hotels, let alone actually spend the night in one. I was told when I was there that a night in a Dubai hotel costs seven thousand dollars!

When people make an overnight transition from the Stone Age to the age of the airplane and the Internet, it is inevitable that they should undergo some kind of internal struggle in the process, and find themselves subject to depression and other psychological ills, especially when they continue to cling desperately to the teachings and social structure of their former environment. Muslims ran before they had learned how to crawl, and tried to climb a ladder they had not even reached.

The West imposed itself, its technology, and its culture upon Muslims by force. It neither respected their individuality nor appreciated their circumstances. At a conscious level, Muslims accepted what the West had to offer them, but deep in their unconscious they rejected it, and it was this vacillation between acceptance and refusal that precipitated the psychological conflict that has destroyed their mental health.

I recently visited Qatar, a small oil-rich Gulf State that is well on its way to becoming another Dubai. As you stroll through its streets you are reminded of California's Palm Springs. You see the population of Qatar shopping in the public markets at all hours of the day, as if they had nothing else to do; the men in their traditional robes, the women veiled from head to toe. The woman walks a few paces behind the man, and she is followed by her servant, who escorts the small children. They proceed like a military convoy, with the utmost organization and precision, strictly according to rank. There are Starbucks cafés everywhere, and these broadcast recitations from the Koran over their loudspeakers. As I sipped my coffee, I heard the following verse: "And He has created horses, mules, and donkeys, for you to ride" (16:8). This verse is still recited even though there is not a single donkey or mule left in the whole of Qatar. The asses and the mules wrestle in the Muslim unconscious with the planes that the West has imposed mercilessly upon their conscious minds, and it is the Muslims themselves who are the victims of this struggle.

God placed donkeys and mules at Muslims' disposal, while the West gave them mastery over new forms of transportation, but they cannot acknowledge the magnitude of the West's attainments, because they regard them as a challenge to the achievements of God. In their conscious minds they have chosen the accomplishments of the West, but in their unconscious it is God's deeds that take precedence and reign supreme. Muhammad could portray the magnitude of God's power to his followers only by persuading them that he had placed the donkey and the mule at their service, so that they could ride on them. They thought about this and said to themselves: Were it not for the power of this God, mules and donkeys would not be able to carry us from place to place, and so they continued to be grateful to God.

When the legions of the West stormed the desert with their modern means of transportation, Muslims left their donkeys and mules to the mercies of the wilderness and accepted the gifts the West had to offer—with satisfaction, though never with gratitude. I know a Muslim woman who lives here in California. She has a strong personality and is renowned for her supreme self-confidence. She has lived all aspects of American life to the full, has been twice married and divorced, and has used the American justice system to ensure that both her former husbands give her everything she is entitled to under the law. I once saw her interviewed by an Arabian Gulf television network. The program's host asked her, "Why don't you cover your head?"

Contrary to all my expectations she replied, "This is an issue that I agonize over, and I lie awake at night worrying about it. I acknowledge that I have acted wrongly with regard to my religion." Then she added, "It is the society we live in that has made us stray from the true religion." Saddam Hussein killed, massacred, and burned his people with chemical weapons and threw innocent people into jail to serve long sentences. He waged war on Iran for eight years, invaded Kuwait and set fire to its oil, and led his people to destruction—yet he never once expressed remorse for what he had done. From the dock he insisted repeatedly that he was Iraq's legitimate leader and that those he had killed had deserved to die. Not a single Sunni clergyman has expressed any regret over what that criminal did to his country.

After Khomeini's Islamic revolution in 1979 the mullahs of Iran destroyed one of the wealthiest countries in the Middle East and brought its people to the brink of starvation, yet they still insisted that God had entrusted them with a mission to defend their religion. No Shiite clergyman has expressed regret for the crimes these criminals have committed against their country. Sunni Muslims criticize Shiite leaders, and Shiites criticize Sunni leaders, not because of any crimes these leaders may have committed, but because of their secret resentment toward the community to which they themselves do not belong.

The concepts of winning and losing have different meanings in the Muslim cultural lexicon than they do in the West. From our earliest youth we were taught that when someone else wins, we lose, and that we win when others lose. My mother was less concerned with my getting a perfect score in all my subjects at school than she was with what grade the neighbors' daughters had gotten. We are not capable of building a spaceship, but I can still recall how we danced and shouted for joy when the American space shuttle *Challenger* disintegrated, killing its entire crew. The tsunami killed hundreds of thousands of people, most of whom were Muslims, yet some Muslim clergymen told us that the disaster was God's way of punishing the unbelievers who filled the Indonesian nightclubs with prostitutes, and began to spread stories of a mosque that had remained standing, unaffected by the storm. The death of hundreds of thousands of people is no loss, so long as we have gained a mosque!

A Muslim friend told me the following joke, which exemplifies the Muslim concept of winning and losing: "God was walking along when he came across an American who was crying. When God asked him what was the matter, the American told him, 'My neighbor's got a Hummer and I haven't.' When God asked him, 'What do you want me to do about it?' the American replied, 'I want you to get me one, too.' God went on his way and ran into a weeping Frenchman. He asked him what was wrong, and the Frenchman told him, 'My neighbor's got a house on the Champs Elysées and I haven't.' When God asked him what he would like him to do, the Frenchman replied, 'I want you to get me one just like it.' God continued on his way until he saw an Arab in tears and asked him what was wrong. 'My neighbor's got a camel and I haven't,' replied the Arab. When God asked him what he could do to help, the Arab told him, 'Kill my neighbor's camel!'"

13.

Living in the "New" America
Thinking About Colin Powell and
President Barack Hussein Obama

ON CHRISTMAS 2008, I celebrated the twentieth anniversary
of my freedom. Two decades had passed since my arrival in
America, but I often felt as if I had never left Syria, and the
pain was still etched deep in my unconscious.

I can still remember that day as if it were yesterday.

It was December 15, 1988, nighttime, and a fierce storm was
beating down on Damascus from all sides. I left my sister's
home in that tumultuous city at nine o'clock in the evening,
bound for the American embassy.

My sister's husband was a high-ranking officer in the Syrian
army, and my nephew refused to drive me all the way to the
embassy in his father's car, which had a military license plate,
because he felt it would be disrespectful to his father's honor as
a soldier to do so; he made me get out of the car when we were
about a mile away from the embassy.

I walked through the darkness, struggling to fight off the
fear and cold that assailed me. My coat provided poor protection against the wild storm, but at that moment the dream of
freedom was stronger than all my sufferings.

I took my place in the long line of people that stretched in front of the embassy, wrapped myself in a tattered quilt I had brought with me from my sister's house, and lay down on the ground to wait for daybreak: perhaps in the morning I would get the opportunity to meet the American official in charge.

In the morning the guard stood at the door of the embassy and shouted out: "Only the first twenty people registered can come in!"

When I realized that I was number eighteen I shouted, "Thank heavens! America's only a stone's throw away from me now!"

My night at the embassy door had not been wasted.

My turn came, and I was interviewed by the embassy official. After she had looked at my papers and listened to my replies she stamped the visa into my passport.

At that moment I felt as if I held the whole world in my grasp. Christians believe that Saint Peter has the key to the kingdom of heaven, but where I come from people believe that the officials of American embassies worldwide are the bearers of that key.

When I came out of the embassy I hardly knew which way to turn, then I saw that my younger sister had come to see how I was getting on and was waiting on the sidewalk on the other side of the road.

I danced and flourished my passport at her, crossed the road without looking, and narrowly escaped being run over by a car. One of the people gathered at the entrance to the embassy shouted, "Congratulations! Fate has saved your life twice— once by rescuing you from that car and once by giving you a visa for America."

I cannot help but compare every moment of my life here with moments I lived through over there. These comparisons leave me alternately happy and sad, bold and frustrated, hopeful and despairing, as the present in all its beauty contends with the ugliness of the past.

I love America as few people do, and my love for it makes me feel concern for it. I do not want any danger to threaten the safety or beauty of this country that rescued me from my fears and fed me when I was hungry.

In the course of my life here I have witnessed five presidential election campaigns. I watched the first four on television without experiencing any profound sense of involvement. Until this most recent election I regarded American politics as a luxury that did not concern me: What I had already achieved was enough to satisfy me emotionally, physically, and intellectually, and anything beyond that was much more than I required. All aspects of my life seemed to me so like a dream that I almost had to pinch myself to reassure myself that this actually was real life.

I came to believe that the might of America was much greater than whatever president—Democratic or Republican—happened to be in power. America is a regime, a legal code and a moral authority—a vast entity that no one can harm. I believed that any person who attains the rank of presidential candidate had to be great, regardless of party affiliation, and that he or she would genuinely be capable of leading this great nation.

Although candidates' policies might differ, I felt an odd sense of reassurance that each of them would do his or her best for this country and that it was impossible that America would produce a person who, after reaching such high office, could prove unworthy of it. Because of this, I never took the trouble to inquire which candidate was the more worthy of victory; for me it was a mere toss-up, and a matter of indifference if the result were heads or tails.

For me America was—and still is—leaving home at five a.m. and making my way to Starbucks for my morning cup of coffee without fear that someone might see me and accuse me of immoral behavior.

America for me means saying "good morning" to my neighbor and chatting to him for a few moments without being accused of having spent the night with him.

America for me means that my daughter can come home and tell me that she's had lunch with her boyfriend without being beaten for having impugned the family honor.

America means I can wear what I like, eat what I like, and go where I like without anyone's interfering in my decisions.

America means I can buy new shoes before my toes begin to peep out of the old ones and that I can buy new clothes without having to deprive my infant son of milk for a week.

America means calling a government office and hearing a polite voice say: "Good morning, this is Jessica, how can I help you?"

America means I can go into a public washroom, find it equipped with running water, soap, and paper towels, and not have to wade through another person's waste.

America means getting smiled at by a stranger just because our glances have met.

America means spending the day with my family in a beautiful public park without getting eaten alive by flies or being surrounded by piles of garbage at every turn.

America means that the stranger who bumps into me accidentally says, "I'm sorry, I do apologize!"

America means I can enter a place of worship and listen to the sermon without hearing other religious denominations being vilified.

America means someone can knock at my door and I can decide whether or not to open it without having to fear for my life.

America means I can lodge a complaint against the policeman with whom I have had a difference of opinion, in broken English mixed with Arabic, and—possibly—win my case.

America means I can speak Arabic-inflected English and people who hear me will tell me, "You do speak English well!" without the slightest hint of mockery or scorn.

America is the hearing aid my son received in the first week after his arrival in the United States, restoring his hearing after nine years of deafness in Syria.

America means that I live in a street with people of nine different nationalities and that, when American Independence Day brings us together in the public area in front of our homes, each of us brings along his or her national dish for the others to taste.

America means I can live my life and no one will judge me because of my color, gender, race, religion, political opinions, or country of origin; instead I am evaluated on my work and my personality.

America, to put it very briefly indeed, is my freedom.

People have asked me in the past, and many more will ask me after they read this book: "Why don't you see America's bad points?" Perhaps I am blind, but I can see no bad points in

America. In order to understand my perspective, of course, you would have to be a woman who has lived in Syria or another Muslim country for thirty years! This is why I never take the plunge into politics and why, up until now, the election of a president seemed to me a mere intellectual luxury for which I feel no pressing need. When it comes to presidential elections, my conviction remains what it was: Anyone in America who manages to become a presidential candidate is a true American and America has nothing to fear from a true American. The events of September 11, 2001, however, have colored my thoughts on this, somewhat, and influenced my way of thinking. It made me wonder how well America understands Islam and the possible consequences of misunderstanding it.

The events surrounding this most recent election have increased my misgivings, and my anxieties for this country that I love with all my heart have grown proportionately. Foremost among these was President Obama's Muslim background. Everyone knows that he was born of a Muslim father, spent part of his early life in a Muslim country, and attended a Muslim school. This was not what concerned me: President Obama's assurances that he is a Christian were enough to allay any doubts I might have had, together with my conviction that any American capable of being a presidential candidate is an American worthy of my trust—and this conviction of mine remains valid today.

Obama's curse, for me, is his middle name: Hussein. Why? Islamists who grasp the true nature of Islam and believe absolutely that they have a divine mission to take over the whole world one day regard Obama as a heaven-sent sign that they are no more than a stone's throw away from realizing the dream they live for. They are engaged in a constant search for anything that seems to them divinely inspired, and read what they seek into things that would perhaps not appear significant to an American.

Once, when I was browsing through a Web site in Arabic, I came across a news item announcing that the American actress Halle Berry had had a daughter on whom she had bestowed the Arabic name of *Nahla* ("bee"). Then I read readers' comments on this piece of news. Believe it or not, a considerable number of readers were jubilant, as they regarded the event as a sign from God that Islam had begun to advance into America, because the word *nahla* is mentioned in the Koran. The Islamists are not particularly interested in whether Obama is a Muslim or not: The fact that the American president bears a Muslim name like Hussein is enough to convince them that Islam is marching into America and has already infiltrated the White House.

Every day my inbox was flooded with dozens of e-mails full of rumors about Obama that reflect some Americans' fears regarding the Democratic candidate's Muslim background. I read most of them, and I won't disguise the fact that they alarmed me; however, they never succeeded in changing my convictions. I had no fears at all for America, during the campaign, about the prospects for an Obama victory. I had every confidence in him during the election and I still do. My fear for America was that a victory for Obama could breathe fresh life into Islamic terrorism because of what his middle name might suggest to those watching in Islamic countries. Still, I was sanguine until the day when I watched an interview with former Secretary of State Colin Powell on NBC's *Meet the Press.*

For me this interview was a turning point. I was shocked by a remark made by Mr. Powell that had nothing to do with the subject at hand. Mr. Powell expressed his displeasure at the McCain campaign's accusations that Obama was a Muslim, and retorted, "And what if he were? What would be wrong with that?" At that moment I felt as if the room were spinning around and I held on to my chair, afraid I might fall. This remark poured salt on my wounds and posed a question: If Colin Powell doesn't know what it means for the American presidential candidate to be a Muslim, then who does? The man who had once held the post of American secretary of state couldn't see what was wrong with America's choosing a Muslim president, even though it is the country that has suffered most from Muslim terrorism and paid the highest price because of it. Until that moment I had considered Mr. Powell one of the giants of American politics. To me he was as majestic as the American eagle. But in that moment, sadly, I saw the eagle topple from its lofty peak and tumble down in front of me like a little bird. And with it tumbled many of my convictions.

I know that Mr. Powell, who lives by the American moral code on which he was nurtured, refuses to judge people on the basis of their religious affiliation, and that is his right. But he does not have the right to be ignorant or to disregard the fact that Islam is not just a religion: It is a political doctrine that imposes itself by force, and we have to subject to microscopic scrutiny any Muslim in America who ascends to the heights of this sensitive and supremely important post.

I would not want anyone to regard what I am saying as anti-Muslim prejudice. Muslims, like anyone other national group, can be either good or bad, and the best among them do not act in accordance with the teachings of their religion, either because they are not familiar with them, or because they have deliberately progressed beyond them; but to understand what it would mean for a Muslim to become President of the United States, one must search through Islamic history—the history of the Arabs, which is my own history—for a Muslim leader and look at his actions.

The first and most obvious Muslim leader we meet in our search is Muhammad, the Prophet of Islam. Had Mr. Powell read the life of Muhammad, as it is recounted in the Arabic sources and as I learned it in my schooldays, he would fall down in a dead faint. In third grade at primary school I read with pride in our religious primer how Muhammad had beheaded eight hundred Jews from the Bani Quraiza tribe in one night, then taken their wives and children hostage, and spent that same night with the Jewish woman Safia, whose husband, father, and brother he had just killed. This is only a drop in the ocean of what was written about the crimes of Muhammad in the Arabic sources, but, unfortunately, Mr. Powell—it seems— has never troubled to familiarize himself with the most malicious enemy ever to have confronted him or threatened his safety. Once Americans understand that the Koran insists that Muhammad is the ideal that every Muslim male should imitate, they will realize that a Muslim candidate for the American presidency is a very serious matter.

If America had used a small and insignificant proportion of what it has spent on the war against terrorism to fund the translation of so far largely untranslated Islamic dogma and history from Arabic sources, it would have saved itself billions of dollars—let alone a great deal of wasted time and spilled blood. America will never win the war until Americans read about Islam from Arab sources, word for word, without distortion or falsification. Reading this material will enable them to draw their own personal conclusions and help them to understand what kind of enemy they are facing. If Colin Powell becomes one of the people who reads these translated sources and sees the hate and violence they contain, he will bite his lips and say to himself: "I was ignorant of the true nature of my enemy, and this was my worst failing."

After the events of September 11th, I watched a press conference with an American general whose name I can no longer recall. In the course of the conference, he declared that he had read the Koran twice, and one of the reporters asked him, "What conclusion did you reach after you had read it?" He bowed his head for a moment before replying, "We have to defend ourselves." At this point I have to ask, "Mr. Powell why won't you stand up and defend us and the country you love?"

President Obama has declared that he is not a Muslim and I believe him; but if he *were* a Muslim, things would be different. I and every other loyal American would have to adopt a different attitude. Islamic teachings include the notion of *taqia* (literally, "caution, prudence"), which allows a Muslim to conceal his true feelings and cherished beliefs when he feels that non-Muslims around him have the upper hand, while at the same time working secretly to achieve his great objective, so that he can attack them when the time is ripe. Naturally, not all Muslims believe in this principle or act in accordance with it, but the painful truth is that the West has to defend itself and try to subject every Muslim to microscopic scrutiny, especially those who are candidates for the leadership of the most powerful country in the world.

No one can be a true Muslim and a true American simultaneously. Islam is both a religion and a state, and to be a true Muslim you must believe in Islam as both religion and state. A true Muslim does not acknowledge the U.S. Constitution, and his willingness to live under that constitution is, as far as he is concerned, nothing more than an unavoidable step on the way to that constitution's replacement by Islamic Sharia law.

The Koran says: "Believers, take neither Jews nor Christians for your friends. They are friends with one another. Whoever of you seeks their friendship shall become one of their number. Allah does not guide the wrongdoers" (5:51). Would a Muslim candidate for the American presidency be able to put his trust in Jews and Christians if he believes they are not fit to be his friends and protectors? This is a question I leave to Colin Powell to answer, and when I get the right answer from him I will be reassured that America is in safe hands.

On November 4, 2008, after a very difficult labor, the American people elected Mr. Barack Obama as their president. That very same day my daughter Farah suffered a very difficult labor, too, and, after exercising my right to vote, I rushed to the hospital to be with her. In the labor ward I was cut off from the outside world for the entire day, and the night that followed seemed very long. I sat beside my daughter's bed holding her hand, trying to alleviate her labor pains.

On the morning of the following day, November 5, my first granddaughter, Jazlyn, was born, and her cries mingled with the voice of Mr. Obama issuing from the television set in my daughter's room. In the excitement of the moment, the words of the news commentators: "This could happen only in America" lingered in my mind throughout the president's acceptance speech. It's true. Only in America could a member of a minority be elected by a majority.

And only in America could a girl be born of mixed races, then acquire a new citizenship totally unconnected with her origins. America is the land of dreams—and what's more, it is the only country where every dream can come true.

I can almost hear the voices of American television announcers forty years from now telling the world: "Wafa Sultan's granddaughter Jazlyn has been elected president of the United States."

Who knows? One can dream, can't one?

And perhaps in that selfsame year muezzins will announce from the minarets of Syria: "Wafa Sultan's efforts have been crowned with success, and a new god has been born: a God who loves."

Until then, I hope and I pray and I fight and, yes, I dream a little.